ROCK • LIVES

THE ULTIMATE STORY

FREDDIE MERCURY &
QUEEN

ROCK • LIVES

THE ULTIMATE STORY

FREDDIE MERCURY &
QUEEN

NEVILLE MARTEN
and JEFFREY HUDSON

Design: Slatter-Anderson
Printed through: World Print, Hong Kong

Photographs: Denis O'Regan

Published by Castle Communications plc, A29 Barwell Business Park, Leatherhead Road, Chessington Surrey, KT9 2NY.

Copyright: Castle Communications plc 1995

ISBN: 1 8607 40 405

AS IT BEGAN

April 20th 1992. The closing strains of 'We Are The Champions' shook through Wembley Stadium and, via a live global TV link up, the world. Liza Minnelli, resplendent in a gravity defying mini frock, had led the crowds and the amassed superstar supporting cast through the final chorus and then it was over. As the various generals of rock's most select armies filed off stage to the strains of 'God Save The Queen', 72,000 fans cheered. But something was missing. Someone was missing.

The Freddie Mercury Tribute Concert For AIDS Awareness served several purposes. It was a celebration of one man's extraordinary life and his sublime musical gifts; a profile hoisting exercise to publicise the wicked disease that had so cruelly ended his life; it also provided an opportunity for legions of fans – record buyers and celebrities alike – to pay their last respects to someone who had changed their lives.

Freddie Mercury the man had passed away in his sleep some five months earlier, the victim of bronchial pneumonia brought about by AIDS. His body had been cremated at a private service, attended by only a handful of close friends and relatives. In the spring of 92 his fans were offered a chance to say farewell in the style and on a scale that he would have loved. It was certainly no more than he deserved.

Freddie Mercury was a phenomenal performer, but then Queen were a phenomenal band. Four graduates well versed in working for results, their ascendancy to rock's loftiest peaks was neither swift nor comfortable. But it happened and, largely, on the band's own terms. Although not much younger than the likes of Paul McCartney and Eric Clapton, and the same generation as David Bowie and Elton John, Queen's rise to fame came relatively late in their lives, at least by pop standards – when they first entered the Top 10 Freddie was already 27 – and they were seen as newcomers by those who were to become contemporaries.

Queen's reign began in 1974 following a performance of 'Seven Seas Of Rhye' on the then relevant *Top Of The Pops*. David Bowie had pulled out at the last moment and something was needed to fill the slot. The band had just completed their second album, *Queen II*, and leapt at the chance to make their first real impact on the media after three years of trying. The show was a success and the song shot straight into the charts. Penned by Mercury it was an audacious blend of swirling guitar harmonies, multi-layered vocals, lyrics of pomp and doom and one of the most distinctive opening piano motifs ever heard. More than two decades later it stands as a classic, untouched by time and as

impossible to categorise now as then.

With that short burst of pure power pop, Queen had arrived.

The roots of 'Seven Seas Of Rhye' are hard to trace. Certainly you would not immediately associate them with a young ex-public schoolboy of Persian descent, but originate here they somehow did.

Freddie Mercury was born on 5 September 1946. Or rather it was Farookh Bulsara who came into the world, the only son of Bomi and Jer. Mercury would not be born – or created – until some two decades later. With Bomi a High Court cashier for the British government, the family was stationed in Zanzibar, and here Freddie was born. His parents were followers of the strict Parsee Zoroastrian faith and so his and his younger sister Kashmira's upbringings were august and staid, although materially very comfortable.

As a civil servant, Mr Bulsara was prone to the stationing whims of the government, necessitating quite frequent moves. When Freddie was aged eight, his father was instructed to move to Bombay, which he did, taking Freddie with him. Never the closest of relationships, it was not to be the bonding experience the boy perhaps hoped for, however; on the contrary, he was despatched to St Peter's English boarding school in Panchgani, some 50 miles from Bombay.

Suddenly the servants were gone, the attention from his parents had vanished and Freddie's easy going island life was replaced with one of order and 'making do'. As a slight, awkward looking child he had no choice but to try and fit in. He flung himself into his studies, coping with everything and excelling at art. Even at sport

---

Main picture (left):
"When I look back on all that black nail varnish, chiffon, satin and that, I think God, what was I doing?" – Freddie

he seemed a natural, proving himself quite handy in the boxing ring and becoming the school champ at table tennis.

As the confidence which had seemed so scarce when he arrived began to show itself in the sports arena, Freddie was working on other ways of being individual in the constricting confines of the school. His artwork attracted quite a lot of attention, but it was through his burgeoning music skills that he looked set to entertain. Having comfortably reached Grade IV on the piano, Freddie knew that music was in his blood; the school choir and theatre company provided amusing outlets for his talents, but only with his first band, The Hectics, did he really get a taste for what was soon going to dominate his life. Sadly only home functions such as dances and parties were witness to the band's performances, but ever the entertainer, Freddie did his best to put on a real show.

It was while at school that Farookh became Freddie, and the acceptance was complete. From impressionable child to confident adolescent, he had successfully tailored his lifestyle around the demands of school life, emerging at 16 with three O levels (in Art, History and English Language) a fuller, hardier person. While never the boarding school's greatest fan, Freddie would later find that his time at St Peter's had taught him invaluable lessons not perhaps on the syllabus. Through adversity his obvious inner belief in himself had been honed to the point of formidable resolution; his sporting achievements allowed a glimpse of true glory at the end of hard fought effort; and the time spent nurturing his artistic proclivities offered the promise of manifold rewards in time. In his own words, "That background helped me a lot because it taught me to fend for myself."

A brief spell at the family's flat in Zanzibar saw Freddie throwing off the excesses of restriction and, like the coiled spring unboxed, attempting to recreate the carefree, indolent life of old, frittering away balmy days with friends. But this idyllic respite wasn't to last. On 12 January 1964, the British government handed Zanzibar over to the Arabs, a situation which made living there increasingly untenable for all non Arabs, British and Indian alike. Evacuation seemed the only option, and so it was that the Bulsara family came to settle in Feltham, Middlesex, just streets away from where a young man, with the help of his father, had assembled a fireplace, some motorbike springs and a few buttons and was attempting to build his own guitar...

Main picture (right):
The combination of PVC and ballet shoes made Fred's image impossible for critics to analyse

"Here's the battered relic!" Brian May holds up for inspection the guitar he built aged 17, with his father, Harold. Many musicians have captured the public's heart through their playing but no one, almost without exception, can claim to have ensnared imaginations the world over through their instrument. But then no one else owns a guitar like Brian May's. Known affectionately as the Red Special, the Fireplace or occasionally even the Chap, Brian's self-built guitar started life as many other everyday items...

"The tremolo arm is one of those things used to hold the saddle bag up on your bike," he elaborates, "and the knob on the end is made out of a knitting needle! The tremolo springs are from a motor bike – I forget which kind, but a friend of mine had loads of valve springs and we used those." The pearl buttons seconded for position markers were the result of a raid on Mrs May's sewing box, but without doubt the most famous component is the neck, as Brian reveals: "This actually used to be part of a fireplace which was being destroyed. It's solid mahogany and I used an oak fingerboard. The mahogany was a very nice piece of wood but it was so old it had woodworm holes. I filled them in with matchsticks and stained it with Rustin's Plastic Coating – there's tons of it on the neck, although it's starting to go a bit now."

For 18 months father and son worked on the guitar in a spare bedroom. As far as possible, all work was done, quite literally, 'in house' with no challenge too great. "Where the neck is sculpted into the headstock," he continues, "I did all that with a penknife and sandpaper blocks, because we didn't have any power tools or

anything. For the binding we used shelf edging but even then I had to make a little jig to cut it down. I couldn't even get any proper fretwire and so I had to make a jig for that as well, to cut it down to size; then I had to make another little one to curve the wire before I put it in."

Pickups were to be the only luxury. It was not that Brian couldn't make them – on the contrary, he had successfully wound some copper wire round a small magnet to good effect years ago – but the results were just not right. In the end he invested in Burns Tri-Sonic pickups although, typically, even then things weren't quite right. "I rewound some and filled them up with Araldite, all except the treble one which I probably should do some day."

And so, a year and a half in the making, and at a cost of just £8, the Red Special emerged. It looked like no other guitar and it played like no other guitar. Many players are remarkable for their distinctive styles (Edward Van Halen and Hank Marvin, for example); others achieve guitar tones indelibly linked to them (notably Mark Knopfler and David Gilmour); but literally only a handful have ever created totally new sounds: Jimi Hendrix managed it, Carlos Santana and Peter Green certainly did, but Brian May and his Red Special possess perhaps the most identifiable sound of all.

Brian Harold May was born on 7 July 1947 at the Gloucester House Nursing Home, Hampton, Middlesex to Ruth and Harold May. Unlike Mercury's, Brian's early years were spent firmly in the bosom of his family and, if it seems dull now, it was still largely as Brian would have wanted it. He had a close relationship with his father, a draughtsman for the Ministry of Aviation and together they shared many hours satisfying each other's urges for knowledge, mechanical and otherwise. As an only child, he was afforded all the attention that perhaps Freddie always longed for. The result: while the singer demanded – and more often than not, got – the initial spotlights, the fledgling guitarist soon accrued his own media attention by dint of his sheer studied thoroughness and unflashy but unavoidable talent.

Music featured strongly in Brian's childhood, and ironically this was the one area where, if at all, he was inclined to rebel. Recognising the boy's inherent musicality, his parents arranged for Brian to attend piano lessons. Typically, although he resented the enforced encroachment on his time, Brian persevered achieving a highly creditable standard (by nine he had matched Freddie's Grade IV). Desire to fulfil his parents' wishes and an innate will to master any problem saw the youngster triumph; it was just not in his nature to fail.

Certainly with Harold on his side, Brian never met a problem that wasn't surmountable. When ukulele lessons led to a guitar for his seventh birthday, he soon worked out how to play it, although he was hindered by the size of the Spanish acoustic instrument, especially the unmanageable height of the strings over the fretboard. No problem. Aided by Harold, he reduced the guitar's action by planing down the bridge to lower the strings' height; notes were now infinitely more attainable for his small fingers. Now the guitar was physically playable, the sound came under scrutiny. Brian was glad to have any instrument, but as a fan of artists like Buddy Holly and The Shadows, his favourite sounds were made on electric guitars. Again, no problem for the resourceful pair. Three button magnets wound with copper wire later and Brian had created homemade pickups. Once fitted, and played through the family wireless, he had an instant electric guitar – despite its unplugged appearance.

Brian's formative years then were driven by desire and accommodation. What he wanted he usually got, either with technical invention filling the void left by strapped finances, or just through good old fashioned, hard work, no better exemplified than in his academic career.

In 1958 Brian's efforts paid off with a scholarship to Hampton Grammar School. One of his many shared passions with his father had been astronomy; the two idled away many an evening hour in fixed examination of the many constellations the night sky had to offer the knowing eye. Hoping to take this hobby one step further, Brian's school subjects were chosen to shape his pastime into a possible career. Seven years later, aged 18, he left Hampton School, the proud and deserving holder of 10 O levels plus A levels in Pure Maths, Applied Maths, Additional Maths and Physics. Now for a real focus; he applied to follow Astronomy at London's Imperial College and in autumn that year was accepted to study Physics and Infra Red Astronomy.

Despite his exemplary results, Brian's academic life was not all work although, given his overwhelming natural reticence, some of his extra curricular activities must have been far from pleasurable. Not only was he an active player in Hampton School's debating team, but his shyness took an extra drubbing when he put himself forward for roles in several school productions, most notably 'The Admirable Crichton' in which he appeared – pre 'I Want To Break Free', remember – as Lady Mary Lazenby!

But most important in his off duty lifestyle was music. Membership of the school choir whetted an obvious desire to sing

Main picture (right):
"I think I strike a lot of people as being introverted. But a lot of people are the biggest big heads in the world under that exterior"

in public, and by the time he had built his own guitar the bug was incurable. With friends Brian got more and more involved in the local scene, in particular attending many gigs by a group called The Others before finally being inspired to form his own band. Members came and went, and names were a problem but eventually certain things became clear: Brian would play guitar, Tim Staffell would sing (and play harmonica) and the band would be called 1984.

Gigs were few and far between, but almost all were memorable – albeit for different reasons. While a spot at Richmond Girls School (where the band's girlfriends were pupils) offered a naive rush for the ambitious novices, their support stint at Imperial College turned up – in retrospect at least! – a quite amazing opportunity. Top of the bill that night? Jimi Hendrix! In the end, Jimi's only recorded words to the group were "Which way's the stage, man?", but nevertheless, 13 May 1967 was a night Brian would never forget.

The band were to appear once more on the same bill as the legendary Seattle southpaw, this time for the special Christmas On Earth show at Olympia. Also featured were Pink Floyd, T Rex and Traffic. The show did not go well: they didn't go on until 5am the next day by which time all their gear had been stolen from backstage.

Despite their increasingly illustrious bookings, 1984 never really looked anything more than a sideline. Intergroup squabbles affected harmony while Brian's flourishing academic success ruined stability and eventually they disbanded.

But far from being a sign of the breakup of Brian's affair with music, 1984's demise presented just a temporary blip in his plans. Indeed, when approached by a very impressed Professor Sir Brian Lovell to continue his astronomical work at the world famous Jodrell Bank, Brian rejected the offer on the grounds that any impending musical success would not be achieved in Cheshire.

It was a courageous decision and one which could, had events not worked out differently, have plagued a frustrated astronomer's remaining days. As it transpired, while plotting the next step on his road to stardom, the aspiring scientist was freer to devote himself to his studies, eventually going on to oversee the construction of observation huts in Switzerland and Tenerife (on an extinct volcano!). But for all his success, Brian never lost sight of his dream

Main picture:
On occasions Freddie was known to bruise himself with his frantic tambourine playing

ROGER TAYLOR

"I saw this notice pinned to the board in Imperial College saying 'Wanted: Mitch Mitchell/Ginger Baker type drummer' and so I replied. Brian wrote me this long involved letter and I went along and met him. I thought he was quite clever – he liked Jeff Beck – and so we agreed to give it a go."

If Roger Meddows Taylor was impressed by Brian, the admiration was certainly mutual. He and Tim had advertised for a drummer to end their problems and Taylor sounded perfect. Apart from obvious playing ability, Roger possessed a knowledge of his instrument that the two men had never appreciated before: "I watched him tuning a snare," Brian recalls, "something I'd never seen done before – and I remember thinking how professional he looked." With the tuning of that drum, the decision was made!

Born on 26 July 1949 at West Norfolk and King's Lynn Hospital in King's Lynn, Norfolk to Michael and Winifred Taylor, the young Roger's life had little obvious musical background, but that didn't stop him getting the bug at an early age. When he was three, his family life was uprooted as his parents, his sister Clare and he took up a new existence in Truro, Cornwall, and it was there, five years later that, like Brian, he acquired a ukulele and taught himself to play.

A group was formed – The Bubblingover Boys – but gigs were few; in fact they performed just twice, once at Roger's Bosvigo School. The life of the band ended when he left that school to take up a scholarship at the Truro Cathedral School. With the thrills of performance still in his blood, he joined the choir; like Brian, it did little to satisfy his desires.

September 1960, another school, another musical outlet. Attending the Truro Public School (as the only day boy, hence his longer hair!), Roger formed his second band, The Cousin Jacks. Success was once again a distant hope, although one worthwhile event occurred: Roger grew bored of playing rhythm guitar during the band's limited gigging schedule and switched to the drums.

The change of instrument was a palliative measure, however, and his original ennui saw Roger eventually leave the group. His next venture was with an act called Johnny Quale And The Reaction who went on to become the most successful of any of the pre-Queen groups. Local bookings were plentiful, especially when the singer left, taking with him the first half of the band's name. As The Reaction, and now with Roger combining singing duties with his percussion, they continued to be a popular local pull, playing as many as three or four shows a week through 1966.

Proving himself the master of juggling time, Roger managed to keep his gigging commitments while still doing well at his studies. One day to be known as the rock'n'roll heartbeat of Queen, Roger's attitude, even in the mid 60s, was one of fun first, the rest second. Fortunately, where perhaps Brian felt he had to apply himself totally to succeed, Roger found himself gifted with the ability to pass exam after exam on just a few nights' rushed

Main picture (right):
Roger's fascination with science fiction led to American artist Frank Kelly Freas designing the band's 'News Of The World' cover – plus Roger's drum skin

cramming the week before. Seven O levels and A levels in Biology, Physics and Chemistry were easily achieved, and so there was little reason to suggest he wouldn't prosper at higher education. Mrs Taylor, now separated from Roger's father, was tolerant of her son's musical exploits, but she never considered them a fitting replacement for qualifications. Mounting a triumphant campaign with his teachers, she successfully encouraged Roger to accept a course in Dentistry at the London Hospital Medical School in October 1967. Once again, physical distance was to end the life of a band. After a year of Roger only appearing with them in his holidays, The Reaction ceased to be.

The band may have died but Roger's thirst for music thrived; all he needed was the right vehicle. At last he was in London, the music capital of the country, if not the world. Keeping his eyes open for the right opportunity, he soon noticed the words of someone else who had forsaken a prosperous life elsewhere for an aspirant existence in the metropolis. When Roger read the postcard pinned up by Brian he saw a way of living the musical life in London that he had managed to create in Cornwall. Fortunately for music fans the world over, he followed it up.

Smile was born.

For two years Smile had quite reasonable success. Their first gig alone set them against one of the few groups who would vie with Queen in years to come for the title of most elaborate show men – Pink Floyd – and on 26 October 1968, they made their stage debut, fortunately on the friendly home ground of Imperial College. Although Brian had finished his degree (collecting his BSc from Her Majesty Queen Elizabeth The Queen Mother at the Royal Albert Hall on 24 October 1968), he took on some tutorial assignments to support his PhD research, thus retaining his links with the college. While the venue was to welcome them many times over the next few years, occasionally throwing them in support of acts like Tyrannosaurus Rex, it was Roger's connection with the West Country which provided one of the steadiest sources of gigs initially.

1969 provided the group with several highlights. A support slot for Yes went smoothly early on in the year, while in February they went on above Free at a charity show organised by Brian's old college. But the most exciting development occurred in April when, following a gig at London's Revolution Club, they were introduced to Mercury Records rep Lou Reizner. He was bowled over by their blend of good musicianship with progressive rock performance and offered them a deal and, in May 1969, Smile signed a recording contract with Mercury Records.

For a naive young band, the deal was a good one; in truth, any deal would have done, so eager were they to get on in the music business. Their enthusiasm seemed to be rewarded the next month when Mercury installed the band in Trident studios to cut a single. Produced by John Anthony, Tim's Earth and the May/Staffell composition 'Step On Me' became Smile's first landmark achievement; now they just had to get it released. Unfortunately, here the fairytale was to go wrong. In August the single was released, but only in America where, amidst no publicity, it failed to sell.

Disappointed but not yet disillusioned, the band pressed on with what they were good at – gigging. The next blow came when again the chance to record reared its head. This time Mercury asked for an album's worth of material; submerged in De Lane Lea studios, Smile delivered. Once again, despite the brimming pride of the band, reactions were far from ecstatic, only this time the poor reception began and ended with the record company; the album was never released.

Main picture

"Crazy Little Thing Called Love was written in the bath"

With this decision, Smile were dealt an unsustainable blow. Several gigs followed, but group feelings became strained; the last thing Staffell in particular wanted to do, or be a part of, at this time was Smile. His decision to leave early in 1970 (later to join Humpy Bong), signalled the end of the group and Mercury's contract with them, but May and Taylor had come too close to living their dream to give up. Like Staffell they too were dejected, but they appreciated the efficacy of simple hard work. They would not make the mistake of giving up again.

Main picture (right):
"I like to have a support. It's nice to go on to an audience which is warmed up, and also if it's a good support it gives you something to work off. We had Gary Moore in Germany and I'd be sat backstage hearing all this going on out front and thinking, Jesus, I've got to go on and follow this guy!"

FREDDIE MERCURY

"Why are you wasting your time doing this? You should do more original material. You should be more demonstrative in the way that you put the music across. If I was your singer that's what I'd be doing."

Freddie Bulsara had some very definite views on Smile's act. He wasn't being vicious; on the contrary, he was one of their most ardent fans as well as being the flatmate of Tim Staffell. But while there was something about Smile he was attracted to, his reservations about their style kept him always on the outside.

Like everything in his circuitous life, Freddie's ingratiation into the London music scene had not been straightforward. His family's flight from Zanzibar had caused all sorts of resettling problems, but as a hardened loner after years of boarding, he responded in resilient fashion. Recognising a sketchy 'survival of the fittest' system operating in his English society that was in marked contrast to the hours he was free to squander on African beaches, Freddie sensibly focused on his own strengths. Quite obviously, he concluded, he should be looking towards following a career in art. Once he had set his sights on something, nothing would stop him and, despite his family's reservations, in September 1964 Freddie began an A level Art course at Isleworth Polytechnic; two years later he walked away with a Grade A qualification.

His next stop was Ealing College of Art. Joining in September 1966, it was here that Freddie's natural artistic bent took a slight deviation as he was drawn by the appeal of music and, in particular, Jimi Hendrix. With typical ambiguity Freddie was later to describe his two greatest influences as Hendrix and Liza Minnelli; for now, the left-handed, Stratocaster wielding genius dominated the young artist's waking thoughts. "He was captivated by Hendrix," Brian recalls. "He invited me round to his house where he had this little stereo and played me some Hendrix. I said, This guy really makes use of stereo; so we went from one speaker to the other, finding out how he produced those sounds." Freddie spent hours painting, sketching and – most extreme yet – impersonating his idol, but it was not enough. There was no going back; art had been a superb outlet for his frustrations, but he had to get into music.

Further incentive came at the college when he met up with Tim Staffell, himself an established band member. Warming to the already slightly eccentric Freddie, Tim took the newcomer along to see his band, Smile, rehearse. The other members were equally attracted to this wild haired, emaciated artist and a life long friendship was struck. By day he would sell (or attempt to!) clothes from a stall in Kensington Market he shared with Roger; by night he would encourage the band.

Watching was all very well, but it was not the same as actually doing it. At that time Smile were ticking along very nicely and Freddie, whose only experience had been with his school band The Hectics, was bowled over by the fact that they were actually playing gigs. With his course completed and a diploma in Art safely his, Freddie had the summer of 1969 free to seek out the right vehicle to fulfil his ambition. It came in the unlikely shape of Ibex, a Liverpudlian three piece band seemingly going nowhere. Their main problem was the lack of a decent singer; enter Freddie. Having taught himself a few basic chords on the guitar, he became the perfect frontman for the group. Rehearsals were many and gigs few at first, but soon they began to trickle in. Unfortunately, whereas Smile's itinerary saw them commuting between Cornwall and London, Ibex's appeal was split between the capital and the north. It was far from ideal, and a decision had to be made. In the end the whole group uplifted and relocated in Merseyside.

It worked for a while, but like Brian before him, Freddie was convinced that real success would always lie in London – even The Beatles had had to make the move! In September 1969 he relocated back to London, richer in experience, more focused on his goal and possessing a microphone technique like no one else's. The latter came about purely by accident. At one particularly catastrophic show at the Wade Deacon Grammar School For Girls, when just about everything else had gone wrong, he attempted to twirl his tall microphone stand Rod Stewart fashion, only for the bottom half to snap off. Ever redoubtable he persevered with half a stand that night – and for the next 20 years!

Back home, the dream looked like fading, but Freddie had other ideas. Auditions became a part of his daily routine for a while, and in late 1969 he won the job as singer with Sour Milk Sea. Sadly it wasn't to last; in-group cliques led to squabbles and eventual disbandment.

Freddie was sharing a Barnes flat with Smile at this time, so the group's evolution was played out in front of him on a daily basis. From his fluctuating position of being in, then out of a group, he grew more and more confident in his criticisms. Brian, Roger and Tim listened, but heeded little; after all, his success rate in bands was not fantastic. However, when Freddie's latest stab at success ended with Wreckage, his current group, disbanding in March 1970, there was a new opportunity, catalysed by the exit of Staffell from Smile...

Main picture (right):
"I suppose my dad only came to terms with me being a rock musician when he saw us play Madison Square Garden. Until then it was, 'That's okay, but you'll have to get a proper job later'"

Picture (above):
"We're pretty proud of what we've done as a whole. We took chances. Some of the things we did set the world alight, and some didn't. But at least we made our own mistakes. We did what we wanted to"

QUEEN

"Smile broke up completely, and we gave up – Freddie was the driving force for getting us back together," Brian recalls. "He told us we could do it, and said he didn't want to play useless gigs where no one listened and that we would have to rehearse and get a stage act together – he was very keen for it to be an actual act."

Freddie's enthusiasm gave Roger and Brian their second wind. Soured immeasurably by the Mercury Records fiasco, they were reasonably jaded although each man was still committed to the dream. With Freddie's help, they saw, they could achieve it.

The first thing to be decided was a name. Ever the flamboyant visualiser, Freddie knew it had to make a statement about the band. It needed to be hard hitting, grand yet mysterious, all at the same time. Roger and Brian came up with Grand Dance (from a CS Lewis novel); it was rejected. Roger suggested The Rich Kids; no. It was Freddie who came up with 'Queen'.

It was not the immediate winner, Brian in particular feeling awkward playing beneath its banner. "But then I realised that if we were bothering to argue so much about it, there must be something in it," he reasoned. All this from a man who thought The Beatles would never get anywhere with a name like that. But Freddie was adamant: "It's very regal, obviously, and it sounds splendid. It's a strong name, very universal and immediate. It had a lot of visual potential and was open to all sorts of interpretations. I was certainly aware of the gay connotations, but that was just one facet of it."

The next step was finding a bass player. Roger's old friend from his Reaction days, Mike Grose, filled this slot, and so it was that the fledgling four piece set out. The results of several months' practice in lecture halls at Imperial College made its teetering debut on 27 June 1970 in Truro. The band were actually honouring a commitment made by Smile – hence some erroneously touted advertising – but this was out and out Queen. The songs were strong, they were well rehearsed and they looked different; on Freddie's insistence the standard rock uniform of jeans and T-shirt was forgotten for striking black and white outfits set off by an abundance of gaudy chains.

When they made their return to Truro the next month things were slightly different. The band was the same, the music was the same and the act remained unchanged. But this time they were advertised as Queen; and Freddie Bulsara had transformed into Freddie Mercury, namesake of the winged messenger of the gods. Things were looking up.

Almost immediately, however, another wave rocked their boat as Mike Grose announced his retirement from music. Sad, yes; a disaster no. Barry Mitchell, another friend of Roger's, was drafted in and with him the band continued its busy schedule of eight parts rehearsal, two parts gig. Things gradually began to pick up, with bookings at Imperial and Liverpool becoming regular towards the end of the year. In fact, the worst event to befall the band in that period, albeit indirectly, occurred on 18 September 1970 when Jimi Hendrix, Freddie's inspiration, died. As a mark of respect, Freddie and Roger closed their market stall for the day.

January 1971: another year, another change round. Barry Mitchell grew bored of the band's studious honing of their act; he wanted results now, so left the band. His replacement, Doug, proved unsatisfactory when he attempted to overshadow Freddie as the focus of the band. He was fired. Fourth time lucky, towards the end of February 1971 they hit upon a young player from Leicester who was quietly working his way towards a First Class Honours degree in Electronics.

Main picture (left):
Queen lasted 20 years without a change in lineup. The chemistry between the four members on stage is almost tangible

John Deacon fitted more perfectly into Queen's hierarchy than he could possibly have appreciated as he played his audition. The previous three bass players had grown disenchanted with the band's dedicated approach to getting things right. They saw it as slow when it was, in reality, measured. As students the members of Queen were used to working towards a goal over several years; in this way they would acquire degrees (or equivalents) in Biology, Infra Red Astronomy and Art. Deacon seemed to fit perfectly into this order of things.

Born on 19 August 1951 at the St Francis Private Hospital, Leicester to Lillian and Arthur, John Richard Deacon's early interests began to prepare his passage into what was to become the supergroup Queen. Given a plastic guitar aged just seven, he knew he wanted the real thing by the time he was 11. When the almost mandatory acoustic had been acquired, he then unknowingly followed in Queen's already established tradition of having to teach himself to play it! Nobody, it seems, had ever heard of guitar teachers!

If the diligence for which he was to become known manifested itself in his home tuition, his later impassive stage presence was perhaps accrued through having to deal with tragedy at an early age. When Mr Deacon died before his son was into his teens, John was mortified; the pair were immensely close, sharing a passion for electronics and amateur radio. Already a quiet lad, he turned even more introspective in his grief, his only outlets being music and study. He had learnt the meaning of pain, and of making the most of what you have; two facets which were to shape him as an adult.

Early groups, The Opposition, The New Opposition and Art (pretty much one group under assumed names!) kept John busy throughout his formative years, with bookings filling up most weekends. During the week, the unlikely superhero of the Leicester rock scene reverted to mild mannered student, easily scooping up eight O levels and three A levels (all Grade As!) by the time he left Beauchamp Grammar School in June 1969.

Main picture

I see a little silhouetto of a man – and his distinctive MusicMan Sting Ray bass

The next stop was the University of London's Chelsea College and an electronics degree, approached with serious dedication in memory of his late father. Music took a back seat for at least a year – although he did go out with a group named Deacon once – until in early 1971 he auditioned for a group called Queen. A background in electronics for all those equipment niggles, a personality guaranteed not to try and upstage the singer, his own amps and guitars all worked in his favour – the fact that he was also no sloppy bass player seemed almost irrelevant as the decision was made: John Deacon became the final member of Queen.

Picture:

***Extreme, Black Sabbath, Bon Jovi, Elton John, The Cross, Holly Johnson, Living In A Box, Comic Relief, Def Leppard, Meat Loaf, Guns N' Roses, Lonnie Donegan, Gordon Giltrap, Bad News** – just a few of the artists Brian has helped out on record or stage*

After so many false starts Queen were now ready to make their final assault on the music business. John's first gig came in July 1971 at – where else? – Imperial College where the reception was good, if subdued. Once again the call of Cornwall proved strong and Queen embarked on a mini tour of a region eager to welcome its musical son. Unfortunately for the rest of the band, the posters reflected their drummer's local popularity, trumpeting 'The Legendary Drummer Of Cornwall – Roger Taylor And Queen', but all in all, things went well.

In September 1971, after several failed attempts at winning VIP interest, Queen's career received its biggest shot in the arm to date. A friend of Brian's who worked for the new De Lane Lea studios mentioned that they were looking for a band to demo the recording equipment for prospective clients; in effect, the band would have unlimited studio time – albeit often with a disinterested audience milling around in the background. "They needed some people in there to make some noise," is Brian's modest recollection of the arrangement. "They were testing the separation between the three studios, and the reverberation times and they wanted a group to do it."

Without hesitation Queen installed themselves in the studios. It was far from easy fitting in around visitors' arrangements, but it afforded them some much needed rehearsal space and – best of all – the facilities to record demos. The results – rough takes of Keep Yourself Alive, Liar, Jesus and The Night Comes Down – spoke for themselves and when ex-Smile producer John Anthony and colleague Roy Thomas Baker visited the studios, a tape was pressed into the men's hands.

The move worked and both men reported back to their bosses, Trident studios owners Norman and Barry Sheffield, with tales of this musical find they had made. On 24 March 1972, Barry Sheffield witnessed an amazing Queen performance and was so smitten he offered the band a contract with Trident Audio Productions. After the Smile experience, things had to be right this time; having already rejected an offer from Chrysalis Records, the band held out for a tri-partite deal with Trident: publishing, management and recording deals or no cigar. They won.

Unbeknown to them, while Queen were being hawked around the various record companies by Trident operative Jack Nelson, it was as part of a package (including a singer called Eugene Wallace and a group called Mark Ashton And Headstone). So, even though EMI actually showed keen interest in Queen, because the brothers refused to let them go without the other two acts, the deal fell through.

Undaunted by their managerial faux pas, the brothers moved the band into Trident's own 24 track studios. The plan was to forget about the record companies for a while; actually make the first album, then do the selling.

As far as the band were concerned, it was perfect. In hindsight, it was far from it. At last they had the opportunity to explore their own musical drives – and on a £20 a week retainer from Trident – but there was a snag. The studios were actually quite busy and the owners refused to turn away paying customers. This meant that Queen's studio time was entirely dependent on whether there was a vacant slot; for the next months they found themselves on call 24 hours a day, ready to rush to the studio at a moment's notice if some recording time became available.

It was by no means an ideal arrangement, having to hang around waiting for the likes of David Bowie and Elton John – both

Queen's age, remember, but infuriatingly an earlier generation success-wise – to pack up and go home for the night, but somehow they stayed at it and by January 1973 work was complete. Queen had finished their first album.

Like most first albums, Queen's début disc drew on songs written over the course of several years. The May/Staffell collaboration

'Doing All Right' obviously came from the Smile period (in fact it was recorded for the aborted Mercury project, later seeing the light of day on a Japanese issue mini-LP), while Liar's origins lay in a song called Lover, co-written by Ibex members Bulsara and Mike Bersin. Put through the punishing Queen machine, of course, little more than the riff made it onto the album.

Although proud of their stage show to the point of worrying as much about presentation – whether via extravagant costumery and makeup or dramatic lighting – Queen's time in the studio had allowed them to expand and experiment musically. Perhaps not on a par with Paul McCartney's famed raiding of the Abbey Road musical stores (he would discover an instrument he liked the look of, get producer George Martin to demonstrate it and feature it on the next record!) Queen nevertheless unearthed an instrument hitherto unfeatured in their act: piano. With two prominently qualified players, they were suddenly transformed from a tight rock'n'roll band into something much grander, with their songs reflecting the broadening horizons.

"A piano on stage at that point would have been impossible to fix up," according to Brian, "so in the studio was the first chance Freddie had to do his piano things. 'My Fairy King' was the first of these sort of epics where there were lots of voice overdubs and harmonies. Freddie got into this, and that led to 'The March Of The Black Queen' on the second album, and then 'Bohemian Rhapsody' later on."

Although competent, Freddie was never a virtuoso player and the piano was never seen as a solo instrument. Brian: "We actually got that sound of the piano and guitar working for the first time, which was very exciting." By example, the album's closer sees that harmony firmly tested as the distinctive opening triplets of 'Seven Seas Of Rhye' tear away (albeit at half the speed of the later single version!) from Brian's chasing guitar. Sadly though, construction strengths aside, the song stands today an inchoate experiment, more a filler than the striking finale it perhaps set out to be.

From the last track to the first, and the band's earliest stab at creating the 'Queen sound'. Written by Brian, 'Keep Yourself Alive' set high standards which some of the later tracks struggled to meet. Lyrically it spoke of an optimistic fight against the odds – typically heartfelt sentiments – while musically the proud opening riff provided just the first of many magnetic attractions. Freddie's voice screamed presence and control (retrospect begs the question: could Tim Staffell have ever coped so well with Brian's material?) and the production was faultless. Brian always saw his instrument as capable of so much more than most players perceived; sure the solo should be the focal point of any song, but there was

immeasurable room for work around the vocals. The results were a full orchestral feel, inspiring many who heard the initial tapes to look for the synthesiser player when in fact the parts in question came courtesy of his own Red Special and a sixpence. (Reviewing its single release in Sounds, BBC DJ John Peel remarked on the "pleasing guitar and synthesiser work"!) When it finally came out, 'Queen' carried the telling legend "Nobody played synthesisers", a statement that was to adorn their first eight releases.

When it finally came out, indeed. A record deal still proved elusive but there was no doubt that things were beginning to happen. A month after the album was completed, Queen were recording again, but this time at somebody else's expense. At the BBC's famous Maida Vale studios they laid down four tracks, 'Keep Yourself Alive', 'Doing All Right', 'My Fairy King' and 'Liar' under the production auspices of Bernie Andrews, for inclusion on the Radio One programme Sounds Of The Seventies. (The same sessions appeared on record for the first time in December 1989 as half of the album *Queen At The Beeb*.) Aired on 15 February 1973, the show was met with a remarkable response; less than a month later, after endless toing and froing of amended contract demands and compromises, Queen were signed by EMI.

The BBC show's success had actually afforded the Trident owners some not inconsiderable clout and, sensing the imminent kill, they pushed for – and achieved – the three act deal they had held out for earlier. Yet again, external wranglings were to thwart the band. EMI's intention had been to sign Queen as the vanguard act of their new heavy rock division, but that division was taking longer to set up than envisaged. Subsequently, the momentum of the radio show, the burgeoning concert buzz and all the industry attention faded to nothing when the album still failed to appear in shops.

In the end it was a very different project that was released. While kicking their heels between recording stints, Freddie, Brian and Roger had become involved in a record being put together at Trident by Robin Cable. The song was 'I Can Hear Music', the old Beach Boys number, and Freddie was approached to lay down a vocal. That done, he enrolled Roger for percussion duties and finally Brian to submit a substitute solo for the original synthesiser effort. With the B-side a version of Dusty Springfield's 'Goin' Back' sung by Freddie, a single was released under the nom de chant Larry Lurex – a parody of the inimitable Gary Glitter. Whether it was Gary's militant fan base denouncing the record, or just a puzzled public querying how you could send up such an obviously parodic figure as 'The Leader', the record failed to make an impact.

Queen's next foray into the singles world was only marginally less disappointing, but at least it was under their own name. 'Keep Yourself Alive' finally became the first official Queen release to hit the shops on 6 July 1973, ably backed by Brian's plodding prog rocker 'Son And Daughter'. The music press were ambivalent. Sounds said "it never really gets going" while the NME, bastion of the hip and trendy, fanfared its arrival thus: "If these guys look half as good as they sound they could be huge." (Ironically, these positions were to reverse over the years. While the NME rarely said as flattering remark as this opening gambit again, Sounds in 1991 awarded the album *Innuendo* a maximum five stars in easily the press's most favourable review. Similarly, Record Mirror's love affair with the band, begun with their view of KYA as "a raucous, well built single", ended with damning reviews of the last studio album proper.)

Despite their success on Sounds Of The Seventies, Queen faced a wall of denial as far as getting the single on the BBC's Radio One playlist. As the country's only national station it held the power to make or break a single; even with BBC Television coverage via The Old Grey Whistle Test, the playlist panel saw fit to reject the song five times.

The album, when it came on 13 July, was to fare only a little better. With no single to promote it, sales were limited. Furthermore, there was the feeling in the media that EMI had overstepped the mark in the sales pitch for their new rock signing and tales of hype began to permeate, thus alienating many in the press.

Hype or no, the band were to find a champion – not for the last time – in a Radio One disc jockey. A decade later he was to be sneeringly dismissive of their achievements (notably on a Top Of The Pops broadcast), but in July 1973 John Peel seemed like Queen's guardian angel, arriving like a deus ex machina to save the day. Despite his station's blacklisting of the single, he was intrigued enough to invite the band to perform a session for his show (a feature still in practice some 20 years later). Recognising the bolstering effect of their last radio appearance, Queen recorded 'Liar', 'Son And Daughter', 'Keep Yourself Alive' and a new track called 'See What A Fool I've Been'.

The music of the first album had of course been ready for some time, although the package as a whole was a recent assembly. For a title, *Queen* was felt to be more direct and therefore more useful to the band than other front runners *Deary Me* and *Top Fax, Pix And Info*. The front cover featured a spotlit Freddie brandishing his mike stand like Excalibur, while the back presented a collage of band snaps through the years (as well as one of the first attempts

ever, from Brian, at achieving the stereo image effect currently the vogue in myriad 'Magic Eye' publications – study the two pictures of Roger's dummy drum kit, Brian assured us, and all will be revealed). As well as the pre-emptive synthesiser denial, the album credits one "Deacon John" – a band joke which everyone but the bass player found funny!

Another sleeve note explained how the album was the result of three years' hard labour. The point was twofold: to elaborate on where Queen were coming from; and to show where they had already been. Part of the album's problem, as far as several reviewers could see, was its lack of fresh identity, but that was hardly surprising given the album's almost elephantine gestation period. "We put on the sleeve that this was the result of three years' work," Brian recalls, "because we were upset and felt that the record was old fashioned by the time it came out. Lots of stuff had happened in the meantime, particularly David Bowie and Roxy Music, who were our generation but who had already made it, and we felt that it would look like we were jumping on the bandwagon whereas we'd actually had all that stuff in the can from a very long time before, and it was extremely frustrating."

Roger's complaints were more specific: "We're called a hype – that's the one thing we're not. We're making it in the old-fashioned way, through selling records, through playing concerts, enabling the record company to get behind you for the second album."

Get behind them they certainly did. In August 1973 Queen were again despatched to Trident studios, this time as bona fide artists in their own right. *Queen* hadn't exactly exploded into the charts but it more than met EMI's and Trident's budgeted hopes. Big things were expected from its sequel – the band had to deliver.

If Queen's memories of 1973 are a blur, then nobody can blame them. Just weeks after their first album's release they were thrust back in the studio to begin work on a sequel. At the same time, under their managers' instruction, they set about filming a short promo film of 'Liar' and 'Keep Yourself Alive' at Shepperton film studios, with Mike Mansfield behind the viewfinder. When the resulting footage turned out to be anything but a viable sales tool, Queen's soon-to-be legendary passion for perfection – whatever the cost – kicked in and they demanded it be reshot, with themselves and the brothers Sheffield at the helm.

Work on album number two swept furiously along. Roy Thomas Baker once again joined the band in the production booth and between them they set about experimenting with every recording implausibility, every long held stylistic ambition and every possible studio boundary. The technical audio restraints that held back so much of the first album's better structural moments were cast off like the restrictive shackles they were. If they could think of something they tried it; the only limitation was their imaginations.

Given the freedom of the studio and as much time as they liked, the band's enthusiasm for real recording in proper conditions saw them whipping through their task like persons possessed. In just a few weeks the bulk of the work was completed and a stack of demos produced. Their alacrity paid off; after all, commitments for the first album were still outstanding.

In September they recorded a show for Radio One's In Concert series, kicking off with a pre-taped rendition of a brand new song, Procession, hot from the studio (the idea of coming on stage to a recorded piece would remain with them until the final tour's One Vision entrance in 1986). Also that month Queen was released in the United States on the Elektra label where it climbed to a creditable 83 on the Billboard charts (two singles – KYA and Liar having made no impact).

Despite these very obvious outward signs of imminent stardom, Queen weren't yet prepared to cut all ties with a practical reality. Brian's natural pragmatism saw him plan for the worst and start teaching English at Stockwell Manor comprehensive in London. He also continued towards his thesis, as well as working part time for EMI Electricals and inventing a programme capable of calculating guitar fret positions to 20 decimal places!

In 1972 John had finished his degree (and begun work on an MSc as soon as possible) and Roger qualified with a degree in biology. And Freddie? Freddie of course continued living the appearance of stardom even if it was without the fiscal backup. "He always looked like a star and acted like a star even though he was penniless," Brian remembers. He somehow maintained his market stall (now with Alan Mair) although his opening hours became increasingly erratic. But then what do you expect from a man soon to be heard declaring "I'm not going to be a star; I'm going to be a legend!"

The 'legend' was soon to be tested on his first national tour. At considerable expense (£3,000!), Jack Nelson had managed to secure Queen the support slot on Mott The Hoople's 20 date circumnavigation of the British Isles, and Freddie in particular knew he had to shine. The press had already begun goading him about his lifestyle and fey mannerisms, but as long as he could cut it where it mattered – on stage – then any criticism fell on deaf ears. "I'd be the first one to respect fair criticism," he said at the time, "but it's when you get unfair, dishonest reviews where people haven't done their homework that I get annoyed."

Main picture

Freddie Mercury in 1982. The ultimate showman

Faced with the growing flamboyance of stage costumes and makeup by now the performance norm, the press found their 'homework' a less attractive proposition than simply hypothesising on the band's personal life, and Freddie in particular soon faced pressure to define his sexuality. He had moved in with girlfriend Mary Austin, manageress of fashion boutique Biba in November 1972, but stage campness led certain quarters to other conclusions. Certainly he had witnessed homosexuality at a young age – at school, of all places – but his own experiences remained a closely guarded secret. "It's stupid to say there is no such thing in boarding schools," Freddie once admitted. "All the things they say about them are more or less true. There were times when I was young and green; it's a thing schoolboys go through. I've had my share of schoolboy pranks. I'm not going to elaborate any further."

Freddie would soon shun press interviews altogether, but for the time being, between issuing such titillatingly ambiguous comments as "I'm as gay as a daffodil", he decided that the best form of communication was through his work. He ploughed his every last ounce of energy into making the national tour a success; the initially wary Mott management were going to be shown that taking Queen on board was no reckless gamble.

Night after night the group went out in front of the elder band's crowd and night after night they left the stage safe in the knowledge that another couple of thousand new fans had been converted. As soon as they made their entrance to the strains of Procession, Freddie began his personal battle to out-thrill every other singer the audiences had ever seen. Dressed totally in black – or white, he was both devil and angel by turn – his striking poses shot rushes of excitement into all who saw him, and with the rest of the band's performances matching him blow for blow, it was often surprising that the headlining act dared to bother to follow them. But Mott were riding high at the time, thanks to David Bowie's intervention in their careers, and they gave as good as they got. Masochists one and all, Mott actually enjoyed the challenge so much that, following the duo's triumphant end of tour extravaganza at Hammersmith Odeon on 14 December, they invited Queen to repeat the billing on their visit to America the next year. Of course they said yes. The year ended with a trip back to Freddie's old stomping ground – not Zanzibar, but Merseyside! – with Queen appearing alongside 10cc and a local band Great Day (which contained two members of Freddie's old group Ibex).

Still buzzing from the success of 73, 1974 looked set to be Queen's year. It started badly when injections for a trip to Australia saw Brian almost lose his arm through gangrene (the visit itself was no better, quickly descending into little more than a Pommie bashing exercise), but things soon picked up. Although chuffed at being voted by Sounds as currently in the top three of Britain's Biggest Unknowns, in February Queen were offered the chance to elevate themselves from that category. When a David Bowie film couldn't be found in time to take its slot on Top Of The Pops, producer Robin Nash looked to EMI for a last minute filler. One of Queen's most ardent fans at the company, marketing genius Ronnie Fowler, leapt at the opportunity of sharing what had been for him an infuriatingly private love affair with the band's music. He said yes immediately; but could Queen do it?

Fowler had a copy of a new track, the barely finished 'Seven Seas Of Rhye', which might do the trick. Unfortunately, although bands mimed on the show in those days, it was never to their actual singles, so a fresh backing track had to be found. With vital hours slipping away, Fowler persuaded The Who's Pete Townshend to give up his recording studio at the shortest notice for the band to get to work on a newer version of the already brand new song. Tired but determined they arrived at the BBC the next day to promote a track that couldn't be bought even if it was the most popular thing on earth!

Mugging mercilessly at the cameras, Queen used their recent experience of filmed shows to stunning effect. Not constrained by the need to actually play, the band threw themselves into performing a chrystallised, three minute advert for their live shows; the fire, the theatrics, the power and – almost overlooked – the music were all displayed for a nation to see.

It worked. The reaction to the show made the response to their earlier appearance on Sounds Of The Seventies seem negative by comparison. Determined not to be caught out, EMI immediately ordered pressings of the song – in its orginal form! – for urgent release. The events of that wintry week make fascinating reading:

February 20, Queen pre-record their appearance; February 21 the show is broadcast (and the band watch through an electrical shop's window!); February 23 and the single is already in the shops.

A combination of the show's massive influence, and Fowler's temporary hi-jacking of the Radio One playing schedules soon whipped up a storm of reaction everywhere. The commencement of Queen's first headlining British tour on 1 March didn't exactly hurt sales either! The press signalled their approval in print (NME gushed how "this single showcases all their power and drive, their writing talents and every quality that makes them unique"); the public simply bought the record.

'Seven Seas Of Rhye' entered the UK singles charts at No 45 on 5 March, eventually peaking at No 10. Of the people who heard it there couldn't have been many who didn't agree that it was two minutes and 48 seconds well spent. The intricate piano intro meant that DJs were unable to talk over the song, ensuring that the full extent of its grand appeal was heard virtually every time. The unfinished piece that had closed the first album was barely visible now, with a searing lead vocal and amassed, sweeping harmonies forsaking the earlier rendition's instrumental stance. A swirling torrent of aural delights burst from radios and record players the land over, audiences marvelling at the lavish production and inescapably strong tune. Everything worked; Brian's incisive and extremely ornate solo majestically stands proud decades later; the musical arrangements still seem fresh; even the fadeout's use of 'I Do Like To Be Beside The Seaside' remains one of pop music's most audaciously self deprecating moments, quelling all possible accusations of pompous pretension before they had the chance to arise (in 1985 they trod similar ground with 'One Vision's' self deflating closing cry of "fried chicken"!). Not bad for a band just setting out on a chart career.

By contrast the B-side was a mere sketch of a song. Due to the rushed nature of the release, the only available – and finished – track was a May composition called 'See What A Fool I've Been'. Closer in style to, perhaps, 'Son And Daughter' than 'Seven Seas', it consequently didn't feature on the final album.

The songs that did make it through the selection process were finally unveiled when *Queen II* was put before an expectant market on 8 March, a week into the tour. In no time audiences learned the words and astounded the group by singing along only days after the release. Delivered in a gatefold sleeve, the front cover saw the band adopt what was to become a familiar group pose, with Freddie flanked on three sides by the others against a black backdrop. The monochrome theme continued inside with A- and B-sides replaced by 'side white' and 'side black', and the counterpoint of tracks called 'The White Queen (As It Began)' on the former and 'The March Of The Black Queen' on the latter.

There could only ever be one 'Seven Seas Of Rhye', but in terms of production, the whole album came close to capturing the sheer opulence of the single. In particular the second side, penned entirely by Freddie, is the aural equivalent of shooting rapids. All manner of mysterious effects, outrageous choral constructions and fabulous orchestrations perpetuate (although once again, "nobody played synthesiser"). Whereas the origins of 'Seven Seas' inspiration were lost with Freddie's death, the creative impetus behind 'The Fairy Feller's Master-Stroke' is beyond question. By taking a painting by the artist Richard Dadd and transferring its characters – Oberon, Titania and Mab and co – into lyrics, Freddie showed a talent for observational songwriting that easily equalled that of another of his idols, John Lennon (it became his For The Benefit Of Mr Kite from 'Sgt Pepper...').

Brian's songwriting contributions took up 80% of the first side (the remaining space falling to Taylor's self-sung 'The Loser In The End'). The most elaborate and 'Brian-ish' song, 'Father To Son', is a heavy, riff laden look at perhaps his own childhood, while the album's opener, Procession, used the year before to announce the band's arrival on stage, offers a feast of multiple guitar tracks mapped onto each other to give the impression of an army of players – the first example of the architectural style that would be forever associated with the guitarist, through later songs like 'God Save The Queen' and 'The Wedding March'.

The uncompromising excesses of *Queen II* meant that it made firmer friends and more bitter enemies for the band than the first album's relative safeness induced. Record Mirror denounced it as "the dregs of glam rock. Weak and over produced, if this band are our brightest hope for the future, then we are committing rock and roll suicide." Glam rock? Certainly. Over produced? Of course! "We were trying to push studio techniques to a new limit for rock groups," Brian opines. "It was fulfilling our dreams because we didn't have much opportunity for that on the first album. It went through our minds to call this album *Over The Top!*"

While the critics were largely put off by the album, it was well received by fans and reached No 5 in the charts (also encouraging a belated interest in the first album which soon climbed to No 24). Many fans still regard the album as the archetypal Queen record above all the others, and it was in fact *Queen II* which allegedly caused the band Extreme to form.

While it is seemingly okay for Extreme to have their heroes, some critics attempted to stem Queen's rise early on by comparing them unfavourably with Led Zeppelin. In all honesty, some of the playing on *Queen II* does owe a debt to tracks like 'The Song Remains The Same', from Zep's *Houses Of The Holy*, but those touches are sporadic at best and Queen never resorted to trying to pass other people's songs off as their own (remember Black Waterside?). Brian: "Led Zeppelin and The Who are probably in there somewhere because they were among our favourite groups, but what we were trying to do differently was this sort of layered sound."

The album's success meant that, although they didn't exactly earn more, Fred finally threw in the towel on his market stall and John finally felt enough confidence in the band's future to discontinue his studies.

On 12 April the band flew to America to begin their tour with Mott The Hoople as planned. It was an exhilarating experience for everyone although the response wasn't as uniformly positive as it had been in the UK. In particular, the black and white stage costumes Freddie had commissioned from designer Zandra Rhodes for their English tour caused eyebrows to be raised. But things on stage went largely to plan, and Mott still found themselves fighting for the right to headline night after night.

Then disaster struck. A month into the tour Brian collapsed on stage at the Uris Theater on Broadway, New York. It was no light ailment either; the doctors diagnosed hepatitis (brought on by his earlier arm infection) and he was confined to his sickbed. The support slot was lost (Kansas stepped in) and the band were forced to return to Britain unsure of when – or if – they would ever go out again as Queen. Things looked bad. Very bad...

IN THE LAP OF THE GODS

Things were touch and go for a time, both for Brian and the band. He was ordered to bed but even then doctors couldn't guarantee a 100% recovery. Nevertheless, he made the best possible use of his time and worked on songs for the next album, due to be recorded in July. With Brian at least able to leave his bed, the band took to Monmouthshire in Wales to rehearse new material at Rockfield studios. They also snatched the chance away from the demands of the capital to write songs and lay down some backing tracks – none of it easy with Brian spending much of his time throwing up in the bathroom between takes.

Work on the traditionally awkward third album began in earnest at Trident on 15 July 1974. Things seemed to be taking shape when, yet again, Brian was struck down, this time with a duodenal ulcer. Gangrene; hepatitis; now this. Following an emergency operation performed at King's College Hospital Brian was ordered to rest totally once more. His enforced lay-off spelled disaster for the group's fortunes as far as he could see, and his recuperation could not have been helped by the fear plaguing him constantly that he would be replaced in the band. He needn't have worried. Far from jettisoning one of their own, the rest of the group simply got on with things as best they could, preferring to scrap autumn's planned US tour rather than entertain doing it without their ailing founder member.

Typically Brian didn't waste the time spent in bed. "I also managed to do some writing," he recalls. "'Now I'm Here' was done in that period. That song's about experiences on the American tour, which really blew me away." Back in the studio he found himself with a backlog: "When I finally got out of hospital there was, of course, a mountain of playing to catch up on, plus the vocal harmonies that needed the depth of the three voices [Fred's, Roger's and Brian's – John claims not to be able to sing!]. We finished off 'Killer Queen', 'She Makes Me' and 'Brighton Rock'. 'Now I'm Here' was started and finished in the last couple of weeks, since I'd finally got my ideas straight for the song while in hospital."

The mammoth workload ahead of him didn't faze Brian; on the contrary, his time on the sidelines had made him more determined than ever that Queen were something special, and certainly worth exerting himself for. "I was able to see the group from the outside and was pretty excited by what I saw," he reflects. "We'd done a few things before I was ill, but when I came back they'd done loads more, including a couple of backing tracks of songs by Freddie which I hadn't heard like 'Flick Of The Wrist', which

excited me and gave me the inspiration to get back in there and do what I wanted to do."

Brian's contributions duly added, 'Flick Of The Wrist', was released as half of a double A-sided single – a fact that escapes even the most keen memories. The reason it is so often forgotten can be summed up in two words: Killer Queen. There was nothing wrong at all with FOTW's vicious tale of managerial corruption set to a suitably breakneck tune; but anything released at the same time as 'Killer Queen' stood to be overlooked! Freddie's tale of a "high class call girl" stormed charts everywhere, reaching No 2 in

Main picture (left):

"This shitty guitar only knows three chords!"

Picture (above):

It's a hard life!

the UK and notching up the group's first ever hit in America ('Seven Seas Of Rhye', released 20 May, had disappointingly failed to chart). Its exotic lyrics, unforgettable melody and outstanding production became the turning point in the band's career. Brian agrees: "It was the song that best summed up our kind of music, and a big hit, and we desperately needed it as a mark of something successful happening to us." Freddie saw it as a mark of Queen's powers to shock: "People are used to hard rock, energy music from Queen, yet with this single you almost expect Noel Coward to sing it."

The song certainly stirred emotions in the fans (who even had their own fan club by now) as Queen shows became increasingly uproarious affairs, with nightly 'high jinx' crowd incidents. On 8 November, the press joined in the Queen party, lauding the band's third album, *Sheer Heart Attack* with ecstatic reviews. The *NME* were particularly glowing: "A feast. No duffers, and four songs that will just run and run: 'Killer Queen', 'Flick Of The Wrist', 'Now I'm Here' and 'In The Lap Of The Gods…revisited'."

The album screamed success, and record buyers agreed, quickly sending it to No 2 in the UK charts. Other standout songs included May's 'Brighton Rock', featuring his concert delay based solo, and 'Stone Cold Crazy'. Roger's track, 'Tenement Funster', features the drummer on lead vocals (continuing the trend of the last two albums) and marks a major leap forward in his songwriting (it was certainly a major highlight of his 1994 solo tour). And, for the first time, John Deacon contributed a song, the poppy ditty 'Misfire'. The whole album effused big budget production, yet after their other release of 1974 it seemed quite restrained. "We did think that perhaps we'd dished up a bit too much for people to swallow on *Queen II*," admits Brian.

Two nights at the Rainbow Theatre (recorded for possible release) ended the UK tour, then came the European leg. Initial haulage troubles aside, it went well with theatres sold out everywhere. Now if only they could transfer this success to America. Both 'Killer Queen' and 'SHA' had been Top 10 in the States, so the signs were good. When the group began their first headlining American tour on 31 January, the welcome was tremendous and they never looked back. Yet again, illness was to interfere, but for once Brian's bill of health was clean. Freddie developed painful throat nodules forcing several shows to be cancelled; nevertheless, the break across the Atlantic had been made: Queen were world stars.

'Now I'm Here', released on 17 January, had kept them in the UK charts, and the tour had made them music press stars in the United States, but Queen were hungry for new adventure. They found it with their first trip to the Far East.

If the crazed mass of screaming fans that met Queen at Tokyo Airport on 18 April wasn't as frightening as anything experienced during the wildest days of Beatlemania, then it must have been close. Queen were No 1 in both the album and single charts in Japan – their biggest success anywhere in the world – and the fans were determined to prove their devotion with some riotous displays of public worship. Their Japanese tour had totally sold out and each show brought with it an ironic trapping of major stardom – new problems for the Sumo security who were often simply overwhelmed by sheer numbers. Very often Freddie was moved to halt gigs while a dangerous crush was averted.

There was no doubt about it. In the eyes of Japan, Queen were the biggest band in the world. It was going to take something really special to get the rest of the planet to agree.

Although the hysteria which accompanied Queen's Far Eastern success didn't translate exactly to Britain, the band – and Freddie in particular – were far from ignored back home. 'Killer Queen' earned Freddie the prestigious Ivor Novello award from the Songwriters' Guild Of Great Britain and the whole band scooped various awards in several music magazine polls.

On the work front, Freddie was offered the chance to produce a young performer called Eddie Howell. The two men got on well so Freddie leapt at the chance of his first extra curricular activity since Larry Lurex (Roger had been the first to work outside of Queen, having done session favours for Al Stewart). Not only did Freddie produce, he also contributed piano playing and some typically over the top, swirling backing vocals and even got Brian to add some guitar chops and a solo. All the Queen trademarks were there and at the end of the session Fred advised Eddie that "if this isn't a hit you should sue somebody". The resulting song, 'Man From Manhattan', was a hit, but sadly not in the UK where, due to the presence of an American bass player on the track, union laws got it banned. The song and album of the same name were re-released by Howell in 1995.

With success outside Queen now established, the only problems were internal: Trident. John had married Veronica Tezlaff on 18 January and needed money for a deposit on a house; Trident refused to loan it. Similarly, applications for a piano for Freddie and a car for Roger were turned down as the managers felt that the band should be able to live within their wages of £60 a week each. They disagreed and a young lawyer named Jim Beach was brought in to get the band out of the contract. By August 1975 he had succeeded and Queen left Trident (at a cost of £100,000 plus 1% of royalties on the next six albums!) and signed directly with EMI. The management gap left was filled by the wily Scottish impresario, John Reid, who was currently managing one of the biggest acts in the world, Elton John.

One of Reid's first decisions was to throw a party in Queen's honour, immediately showing himself as a man after the band's heart. At the bash Queen were presented with various precious metal discs in recognition of sales figures world wide, plus one other less obvious distinction – the Carl Allen award for their outstanding contribution to ballroom dancing!? Nevertheless, the party showed their new manager's faith in them. After years of being told the cash wasn't available, Queen were suddenly surrounded by the means to do their work properly. They took every opportunity to make it worthwhile, and in October 1975, rewarded their trusting manager with the first fruits of his reign, a six minute musical amalgam of every style from rock to opera. Its name? 'Bohemian Rhapsody'.

He was far from impressed; not by the song, that was fantastic. But he was a practical man. He knew that any track over three minutes struggled to get air play on the radio; at twice that, Bo Rap was likely never to get played at all. The band were caught between logic and instincts. In the end they were persuaded by a good friend of Freddie's, the disc jockey Kenny Everett. He loved the song when he heard it at the studio and begged for a copy for his own private use. He also happened to be presenting two radio shows that weekend and, despite reproaching his own weakness each time, managed to play the song 14 times in two days.

On 31 October 'Bohemian Rhapsody' was finally released as a single in its entirety (B-side, a future concert favourite from Roger called 'I'm In Love With My Car'). Crafted in sections, the track was the singer's creation from day one. "Bohemian Rhapsody was Freddie's baby from the beginning," says Brian. "He came in and knew exactly what he wanted. The backing track was done with just piano, bass and drums, with a few spaces for other things to go in. Freddie sang a guide vocal at the time but he had all his harmonies written out, and it was really just a question of doing it."

The question of "doing it" was not that easily answered as producer Roy Thomas Baker remembers.

"It wasn't all recorded in one go. We did the whole of the first section and the rock section, and for the middle part we just hit some drums now and then – after which it was basically edits. We

Main picture (right):

Freddie's cloak for We Will Rock You was designed by Diane Moseley

just lengthened the middle section depending on what vocals were put in, because Freddie would walk in and say, We'll stick some Galileos in here...

"The backing track was done over a two day period. The opera section was done over a seven day period of a least 10 to 12 hours a day continual singing. Then there were all the guitar overdubs and getting on for two days to mix it. I'd say that track, on its own, took getting on for three weeks, because it's three songs merged together to make this one track."

The song's melding of styles led some to see it as little more than a joke, but Freddie was deadly serious. "A lot of people slammed 'Bohemian Rhapsody'," he said later, "but who can you compare that to? Name one group that's had an operatic single."

Point taken, of course. The actual recording of the song was as complicated as its structure. Freddie: "We wanted to experiment with sound. Sometimes we used three studios simultaneously. 'Bohemian Rhapsody' took bloody ages to record but we had all the freedom we wanted and we've been able to go to greater extremes."

Having taken the risks to get the song out, the band needed to ensure it got heard. New touring commitments would prevent them from playing the track on Top Of The Pops so a solution had to be found. It came in Bruce Gowers. Bruce had recorded the band's gigs at the Rainbow and now agreed to make a short promotional film for the song at Elstree where the band were rehearsing for the tour. The film saw them recreate the pose used for the cover of *Queen II* (later revamped for 'One Vision') and showed a kaleidoscope of hundreds of different shots as the mammoth operatic section was restaged. Somehow they had to convey the sheer size of the production – some task considering up to 180 vocal parts feature at any one time! The film took just four hours to make, a day to edit and cost a mere £4,500 but its value would turn out to be incalculable.

As many people talked about the video as about the song. It was revolutionary; it was bold; above all it was good. With its help,

Main picture (left):

12 July 1986.
A-wop-bop-a-lu-bop-a-wop-bam-boom,
the notorious rock'n'roll medley

The less than auspicious début placing of 'Bohemian Rhapsody' at 47 was soon forgotten and the song leapt to the top slot, becoming Queen's first UK No 1 (it was to remain at the top for a record breaking nine weeks).

Their second top hitter was soon to come. Drawing its name from a Marx Brothers film, 'A Night At The Opera' became notorious even before its 21 November release. A special preview had seen the opening track, the snarling 'Death On Two Legs (Dedicated To...)', alleged to be about Queen's now ex-managers (it featured the line "You've taken all my money", for instance). Queen kept quiet, but given Freddie's comments at the time – such as "as far as Queen are concerned our management are deceased. One leaves them behind like one leaves excreta. We feel so relieved!" – EMI felt it safest to pay the Sheffields an early settlement to ward off potential larger suits further down the line.

The rest of the album was less controversial but just as remarkable. *Melody Maker* were legibly stunned: "The overall impression is of musical range, power and consistently incisive lyrics." The probing lyrics can be attributed to the first track of course, the power to any number of songs from the pounding 'Sweet Lady' to 'Bohemian Rhapsody', while the musical range is the understatement of the year. Following the rag bag collection of styles on 'Sheer Heart Attack' (rock, pop and even the do-wop of 'Bring Back That Leroy Brown') its follow up gave new strength to the word diversity. 'Bohemian Rhapsody' donated opera; 'Seaside Rendezvous' threw up a kitsch 20s singalong; 'Good Company' offered skiffle to 39's country/folk; 'Love Of My Life' became Queen's landmark ballad and 'You're My Best Friend' was just pure pop. There wasn't a musical genre Queen couldn't make their own.

It was no accident, as Freddie admitted at the time: "There were a lot of things we needed to do on *Queen II* and *Sheer Heart Attack* but there wasn't space enough. This time there is. Guitar-wise and on vocals we've done things we've never done before. We've surpassed everything we've done before musically."

If the album sounded good – and nobody would argue against it – it was not through luck. On its release it was announced as the most costly album ever. What EMI splashed out in hard cash, Queen matched in effort, utilising five different studios in the recording process. For Freddie's beautiful ballad 'Love Of My Life' it was decided that a different instrument was needed to finish the track off, and a harp was picked. The next step for most groups would then have been to find a harp player, and this in a sense is what they did – except rather than look outside the group, Brian decided to have a go. A suitable instrument was found,

Brian spent 12 hours tuning it, then recorded the two minutes we hear on the song. Extravagant, yes; but a definite sign that Queen meant business.

Another virtuoso performance from Brian is seen on the album's closing track, their version of 'God Save The Queen'. Fans had started singing it at shows the previous year and so this version had been cut to end the concerts; it now ended the album. The effect was in the same vein as on 'Procession', with guitar mapped onto guitar mapped onto guitar used to create a full orchestra of the instrument playing the one song. Naturally the "no synths!" banner remained on the back cover. The front of the sleeve, meanwhile, consisted of a design penned by Freddie two years earlier. He had taken each member's star sign – a crab, two lions and a virgin – and incorporated them into a stunning crest featuring a phoenix rising from a 'Q'. This created a visually distinctive logo that the band would use for years to come.

Both the album and single saw the new year in at the top of their respective UK charts; each faired well abroad, earning high Top 10 placings in the USA, but Britain definitely belonged to Queen that Christmas. To mark the fact, their UK tour climaxed with a show at the Hammersmith Odeon (now Labatt's Apollo) which was broadcast live on BBC television's Old Grey Whistle Test. To cap it all, 'Bohemian Rhapsody' won Freddie another Ivor Novello award.

1976 saw little let up in the band's success. They soared to victory in various readers' polls and enjoyed endless weeks of chart domination. Riding the high crest of a very tall wave, the Queen roadshow was taken to America for their third visit (their second as headliners); it was an astounding success. That success was magnified during a short trip to Japan where Queenmania still reigned unabated; the feelings were reciprocated as Freddie's love affair with the country and its culture became more pronounced. Finally, the tour took them to Australia, where they successfully put the horrific memories of their last trip behind them. All in all, their best start to a year yet.

Main picture (right):

Don't believe in Peter Pan, Frankenstein or Superman

Queen returned to England in May to begin sessions towards their next album, and for Brian to tie the knot with long time girlfriend Chrissy Mullen on the 29th of the month. With the next album already under way, another single was released from *A Night At The Opera* to keep them in the public eye for a while longer. 'You're My Best Friend', only John's second song for the group, was released on 18 June to rave reviews, most notably from *Sounds*: "It'll be an absolute smash, beautiful harmonies, strident guitar chords and Freddie in superb voice. Instant No 1!" It didn't quite make the top, but Queen were happy to settle for No 7 with their first ballad single release.

As work for album No 5 cracked on apace, Queen felt the call of the stage firing them once again. They'd only played to foreign crowds so far in 76, and it was time that their home fans got a chance to see the full might of their cosmopolitan powers in reward for their staunch support. The most efficient route, it seemed, was through picking a large venue. This they did: Hyde Park would be the location, 18 September was the date and the show would be free as a thankyou to fans. Virgin Records boss Richard Branson was approached to help wade through the labyrinthine red tape (his assistant, French born Dominique Beyrand, attracted Roger's eye and they soon became an item) and after all the necessary concessions about safety and scheduling had been agreed to, permission was given.

Two other venues were chosen as build ups to the London show. Queen played two nights at the Edinburgh Playhouse and then an amazing gig in the historic grounds of Cardiff Castle. Unfortunately, the Welsh weather's penchant for dampening such occasions refused to make an exception for Queen and the whole show went ahead in very wet – and by now for the fans, muddy – conditions. But the 12,000 strong audience didn't seem to notice the rain as the band poured their hearts into making it a day to remember.

The dress rehearsal completed, the big day arrived. Between 150,000 and 200,000 people packed out London's most famous park in the biggest free festival there since the Stones' show of 1969. The atmosphere was electric as the lights dimmed and the opening notes of 'Bohemian Rhapsody' rang out in the September night. Unfortunately, due to police regulations and delays earlier in the day, the band ran out of time for an encore; Freddie was actually threatened with arrest if he tried to return to the stage!

As well as trotting through the old favourites, Queen had treated fans by slipping in a couple of new songs from their next album. 'You Take My Breath Away' saw Freddie exposed at the piano, performing a remarkable ballad of personal intensity, while the rest of the band took a well earned rest. The night's other début saw everyone on stage for a rousing new song entitled 'Tie Your Mother Down.' Penned by Brian (possibly about his newly acquired mother in law!), its spiteful lyrics call for a girl's entire family to be shut out while he entertains their daughter, and all to one of the guitarist's most infectious tunes so far. The crowds loved it, and were soon

Main picture (left):

John's 'Another One Bites The Dust' topped the American black, pop and rock charts

screaming out the chorus with the band. Almost 20 years later, the song remains a band and audience favourite; chances are, if you can get Brian on a stage with a guitar, that's the song he'll play.

Both songs, plus eight others, were finally committed to record as the new album was finished in October. After four albums with Roy Thomas Baker, this was to be the first produced solely by the band (although they did work with him that year on Ian Hunter's solo LP *All American Alien Boy*, even contributing backing vocals to a track called 'You Nearly Did Me In'). Whether due to the lack of outside input or not, for the first time in their careers the band seemed to have reached an evolutionary impasse musically, with more than one accusation of 'going through the motions' levelled at them.

Certainly critics had a point: the album's title, *A Day At The Races*, once again drew from a Marx Brothers film (Groucho Marx this time sent a congratulatory telegram and later invited them to tea!), and the cover was the same basic Queen crest (although a slightly new design) only this time on a black backdrop. And yes, with all the moulds having been broken already, production techniques didn't exactly bowl anyone over with their originality this time around. Where *A Night At The Opera* closed with the orchestrated power of the national anthem, its sequel emulated the style, with a crescendoing climax courtesy of Brian's guitar. And while the extra burst of 'You Take My Breath Away' which occurs after the song has already 'ended' is a good touch, its efficacy is dampened by the same trick being employed on the very next track, the country style 'Long Away' (itself remarkably similar to '39', both written and sung by Brian). While not exactly admitting anything, Brian later acknowledged the problem: "I wish in some ways that we had put *A Night At The Opera* and *A Day At The Races* out together because the material for both of them was more or less written at the same time. And it corresponds to an almost exactly similar period in our development so I regard the two albums as completely parallel. The fact that one came out after the other is a shame because it was looked on as a follow-up, whereas really it was sort of an extension of the first one."

Unperturbed, the band and record company threw themselves into promoting the new record before and after its release on 10 December. In recognition of the title, Queen had sponsored a horse race at Kempton Park – called the Day At The Races Hurdle – with all four members backing the eventual winner, jockey John Francombe on Lanzarote. Soon after, Freddie and Roger hand delivered a white label of their next single to Kenny Everett (more originality!) in the hope that he could repeat the same success he had generated for Bo Rap.

Whether or not Everett actually helped at all, when 'Somebody To Love' was released on 12 November (complete with video from Bruce Gowers) it shot straight into the charts at No 4 (a feat not matched by the band until 1984's 'Radio Ga Ga'), finally peaking at No 2. Yet again they couldn't make the Top Of The Pops studios which saw the song being 'interpreted' by the show's resident dance troupe Pan's People. The song itself was another Mercury classic, with Freddie once again dipping into music's rich sack and pulling out another style ready to be subjected to the Queen treatment. Those anticipating a reheated rock opera were disappointed – this time it was rock gospel! (At Milton Keynes in 1982, Freddie would later summon up the spirit of Aretha Franklin and effect a faintly negro accent before performing the song!)

By the time the album did appear in the shops, advance orders had clocked up half a million already. And for all the talk of ideas being lacking, there really were some stunning moments of originality on the album, as testified by the first single. Another Mercury composition, The Millionaire Waltz took the band further up orchestral avenues (replete with triangle from John) while Brian's 'Teo Torriatte (Let Us Cling Together)' had a chorus sung in Japanese (the song was later used by Brian as an encore for the second leg of his Back To The Light solo British tour in 1993).

In the end, there was one aspect of *A Night At The Opera* that its sequel openly sought to emulate – its success. It achieved its wish, and so Christmas 1976 saw Queen end the year as they had begun it: at the top of the album charts where they belonged. But with the new punk force rising in British music, calling for an end to the stronghold of bands like Queen, what would the next year hold?

Main picture (left):

Despite repeated rehearsals for Tavaski Szel, Freddie still had to write the words on his hands for the Nepstadion gig

CHAMPIONS OF THE WORLD

At the close of 1976, Queen pulled out of an appearance on the television show Today at the last minute. Their slot was filled by a young band led by the colourfully monikered Johnny Rotten and Sid Vicious. The group were called The Sex Pistols and they made history that night with their outrageous antics and language on live TV. For a band sworn to end the grip of such dinosaurs as Led Zeppelin, The Who, Genesis and Queen on the rock world, it was ironic that they were soon signed to EMI, home of some of the largest names in the industry; it was even more ironic that the next single pressed by EMI after 'Somebody To Love' was The Sex Pistols' 'Anarchy In The UK'.

For a while Queen's reign continued unworried by the upstarts' claims. Where punk sought to identify with 'the kids' on their own level (apparently achieved by spitting in fans' faces at gigs!) Queen's popularity was founded on the belief that people want to be entertained, with bigger and better gestures. With that in mind, the band returned to America in early January for their most extensive tour of the States to date, this time taking with them another bunch of upstarts keen to make an impression. Having groups like Thin Lizzy as support would have worried most people, but Queen took it in their stride, eager to earn their right to headline on a nightly basis (now they knew how Mott must have felt following them!). Of the many highlights, the night they stepped out in front of a packed Madison Square Garden must surely be remembered, as must their appearance at LA's famous Forum. Things don't get much better than this!

Back home, 'Tie Your Mother Down' was released as a single (Mr

Gowers was flown out to record the video in America), but it only reached No 31. Meanwhile Japanese fans, as a thankyou for their unswerving adoration, were treated to 'Teo Torriatte' as the single in their country.

After the American tour the band took a well deserved rest, although Roger soon got itchy feet and began work on a solo project that perhaps wouldn't fit into Queen's style. Then it was back on the road, this time through Europe, culminating in the UK as Queen Elizabeth II's Silver Jubilee celebrations hit top gear. Now more than ever, going out with Phil Lynott's group seemed perfect: after all, what could be a better draw than the Queen/Lizzy tour! Not content to leave the symbolism there, when the group finally hit London's Earl's Court, they unveiled their new state of the art lighting rig known as 'the Crown', fittingly donating all profits from their second show to the Jubilee fund.

In May the band released their first EP in the UK, cunningly entitled Queen's First EP. Press reaction was unfavourable, citing the ploy of picking one track from the last four albums ('White Queen', 'Tenement Funster', 'Death On Two Legs' and 'Good Old Fashioned Lover Boy') as an unnecessary expense for fans when new material should have been the order of the day. Sounds are succinct in their vilification: "Enough to make one paint 'art rock sucks' on a T-shirt. Destroy!" New material wasn't long away, however, at least not from one member of the group. August saw Roger's solo effort, a cover of The Parliament's 'I Wanna Testify' released, although despite his performance on Marc Bolan's TV show, it failed to chart. Brian meanwhile busied himself contributing to Lonnie Donegan's *Putting On The Style* album (on the songs 'Diggin' My Potatoes' and 'Rolling Stone').

As for Queen material proper, that wasn't far off either. July to September was spent working on a new album at Basing Street and Wessex studios where, ironically, their nemeses were ensconced next door recording their infamous hit *Never Mind The Bollocks Here's The Sex Pistols*. Never one to let down an expectant audience, Freddie excelled himself when confronted by one of the band, as Roger remembers: "One day Sid Vicious stumbled in and

Main picture (right):

The King of Slane Castle, 1986

yelled at Freddie, Ullo, Fred – so you've really brought ballet to the masses then? Freddie just turned round and said, Ah, Mr Ferocious, well we're trying our best, dear!'" That time aside, the rest of the recording went without incident and on 7 October, the double whammy of 'We Are The Champions' and 'We Will Rock You' was unleashed on a slavering public.

The press hated it. "Grisly monomania from Mercury's crew," trilled *Disc*; "Sounds like it's intended to be adopted by football fans all over the country, making it an instant hit on the terraces. Not a bad idea for a load of balls," wailed *NME*. No matter, it soared to No 2 (again – the band's third penultimate slot) in the UK and reached No 1 on America's Record World chart (although Billboard had it down as No 2). Many radio stations, in the US in particular, played the two songs as one track with 'Rock You' leading off (an order adhered to in concert). France went one stage further: 'We Will Rock You' was selected as the main track, going on to notch up a record breaking 12 weeks at the top of the charts, only to be replaced there by 'We Are The Champions' (the songs were switched due to French law restricting No 1 status to three months). This time around the video was shot by Derek Burbridge, who perfectly captures Champions' anthemic mood by focusing on the band's relationship with its audience, with much scarf waving present.

If the so-called rock dinosaurs were finished in the music business, then nobody told the British Phonographic Industry who, on 17 October awarded Queen the unique prize of Best Song Of The Last 25 Years to 'Bohemian Rhapsody'. Never ones to rest on their laurels, Queen celebrated the accolade in the only way they knew how – by releasing a new album 10 days later.

News Of The World was its name, home to 11 highly distinctive new Queen songs and a very disturbing cover. Following Freddie's hold on recent sleeve ideas, Roger came up with this one after being impressed by a picture in the American sci-fi magazine Astounding Science. He contacted the artist, Frank Kelly Freas, who agreed to adapt his horrific scene of a robot clutching dead bodies to include the band.

The album's contents were less shocking, but just as memorable. Once again Roy Thomas Baker was nowhere to be seen near the production desk, but this time the band seemed to have a direction. There's a raw quality to much of the album which stands out, although whether it is the result of a band decision to de-frill their excesses or just the outcome of Fred's increasing boredom with studio life, is anyone's conjecture. Even the cover is pared down: the amusing titles awarded on the previous two sleeves (Fred was first accredited "Bechstein Debauchery" then

"Choir meister, tantrums" while Brian's job description ranged from "guitars and orchestral backdrops" to "Leader of the Orchestra") are missing, as is the "No synths" disclaimer (even though the synths still are missing as well).

The sleeve's economy is reflected in the music. 'We Will Rock You' with stomping rhythm, performed entirely by foot stamps and hand claps, pounds away behind Fred's gutsy reading of Brian's hard hitting lyrics before the guitarist carves up the a cappella action with a no nonsense solo (so successfully remixed by Rick Rubin on the Hollywood Records remastered 'NOTW'). Then comes 'We Are The Champions', Fred's concert tour de force, to add high impact piano riffs to the band's singles repertoire. Of the remainder, two songs stand out: one, It's Late, because it's as overblown and powerful as you'd hope and "as close to typical Queen as you can get" according to Brian; the other, for its simple, poignant blues – Melancholy Blues, in fact.

Remove those tracks and you are left with another legacy of Fred's disillusionment with the constant grind of tour/album: for the first time the group's minor writers get two songs each, while Fred's contribution is less than Brian's. No one is going to doubt John's ability to write a classic song, but 'Who Needs You' was never going to qualify; 'Spread Your Wings', on the other hand, is a chant-a-long in the Fred tradition. Of Taylor's pair, 'Sheer Heart Attack' forces the group along the path half beaten by punk – only Queen play their instruments too well – while 'Fight From The Inside' is more basic rock.

Freddie's diminishing input aside, the album reached No 4 in the UK, but once again external effects were taking their toll. The bigger Queen became, the more attention they demanded and deserved, especially from their manager. With Elton John his obvious priority, John Reid was seen to be decreasing in utility for the band, and so the decision to part was taken. The split was an unacrimonious one, with the severance forms signed in the back of Freddie's Rolls-Royce during the shoot for the video to 'Spread Your Wings'. It was amicable, but expensive: 15% of all future earnings of albums already released were to be paid to Reid. With a pared down core organisation consisting of day to day manager Pete Brown, lawyer Jim Beach, tour manager Gerry Stickells and businessman Paul Prenter, Queen were ready to face the next step in their career.

Main picture

John's Fender Precision bass keeps the low end of Queen in check

November 1977 saw Queen take on their second US tour of the year. Still riding high on the strength of 'Champions', and their first US platinum award winning album, Queen pulled out all the stops, this time, like Led Zeppelin, travelling in their own private jet. They even managed to bring a scaled down version of the Crown from the UK to give American fans a taste of a real Queen show.

The tour was an astounding success, with the new material and Fred's increasingly lavish stage costumes going down well. Spare time activities were a hit as well; Freddie was able to catch his idol Liza Minnelli's stage show and – most importantly – shop, as well as finding time to visit an exhibition by Frank Kelly Freas. The only hiccup of the whole tour came when a 'merry' John needed 19 stitches in his right arm after putting his hand through a plate glass window.

The tour ended at Christmas and with the start of the new year came further changes in the group's managerial structure. Queen Productions Ltd, Queen Films Ltd, Queen Music Ltd and abroad, Raincloud Productions Ltd were formed in an attempt to streamline the band's organisation and keep as much of their earnings for them. Jim Beach became business manager; Peter Chant became tax advisor.

One of Chant's first edicts was to suggest a year of exile for the band: if they spent fewer than 300 days a year in the UK they would not be liable to pay the country's crippling tax rates. On top of that, the next album should be recorded in two countries – neither of them Britain – to ward off foreign tax bills.

The first leg of exile commenced in April with the year's two month European tour, including just four dates in the UK (where they were presented with various Best Group awards by daily newspapers). Almost immediately afterwards, John and Roger set off for Mountain studios in Montreux, Switzerland to fulfil their days quota. Brian arrived later, after his son Jimmy's birth on 15 June (John and Veronica had had their second child, Michael in February), while Freddie stayed in the UK to work on close friend Peter Straker's album *This One's On Me*.

While the album cost Freddie dearly both in money – he invested £20,000 of his own cash in the project in a typical display of generosity – and in vital UK days, one positive thing did arise and that was the healing of any rift with Roy Thomas Baker who co-produced the album. Freddie was so inspired by the old chemistry that Roy was flown out to work on the new Queen album as well.

Phase two of recording took place at SuperBear studios in Nice, France, situated on part of the route of the famous Tour De France bike race. Ever one for way out inspiration, Freddie was moved by the sight of the pedalling mass to write a song called 'Bicycle Race' as his tribute. A series of near random rhymes surrounded the track's basic tenet of wanting to ride a bicycle, while the inclusion of an orchestrated section of bike bells demonstrated that Queen's sense of humour hadn't deserted them after the accusations of taking themselves too seriously still kept coming. In case the sense of humour point wasn't clear enough, someone (no one remembers who!) decided that the song should be a double A-side with a raucous number of Brian's called 'Fat Bottomed Girls', and that there should be a video of naked girls on bikes! What may have started out as a joke soon became fact, as 65 naked women were filmed cycling round Wimbledon Stadium.

For the purposes of the video, the shots of the obliging pedal pushers were kept to a minimum and distorted beyond recognition, making it look more like an expensive prank (its costs escalated further when Halfords insisted the band pay for new saddles on all the bikes they'd hired). The single was released on 13 October, and provoked further controversy with its sleeve featuring the rear view of one of the video 'stars'. The press deemed it childish, but the song still reached No 11 in the UK.

The single barely out and the band were back on tour in America, this time with a new, even larger lighting rig known as 'The Pizza Oven'. Yet again, audience reaction was fantastic and venues were sold out everywhere. The tour's highlight came in New Orleans with the pre-launch party for the completed new album. Among the 400 guests were several speciality acts ranging from fire eaters

Main picture (left):

Brian plays three guitars on 'Crazy Little Thing': this Gibson Chet Atkins, nylon strung acoustic, his black Telecaster for the solo and the Red Special to finish

to strippers to unicyclists, all determined to give the record a memorable start in life.

The new album finally emerged in Britain on 10 November. The cover was another black and white affair, with a pattern of discs providing an eye dazzling image, while the title, *Jazz*, concerned a lot of fans who feared the band's taste for new styles had consumed them. They need not have worried, as both the title and sleeve idea were inspired by a piece of graffito spotted by Brian and Roger during a visit to East Berlin the previous year; the music, of course, was pure Queen.

It was indeed Queen, but with a twist. The previous album's prudent reaction to the earlier releases' epic production were nowhere to be seen. What the reunited team of band and producer managed to convey was a sense of cosmopolitan vitality, reinstating their recently absent feeling of enjoyment in making music. The first singles make the point, and it is reaffirmed in the lyric to Roger's stark rock out 'Fun It'. Still on the flippant side, Freddie's autobiographical (with the emphasis on graphic) account of life on the road is rattled through in the vibrant 'Let Me Entertain You'.

The upbeat feel continues in John's 'If You Can't Beat Them' and Brian's riff laden 'Dead On Time' (the latter complete with "thunderbolt courtesy of God"), but Fred eclipses all with his superb 'Don't Stop Me Now'. After a piano intro, the song leaps into life with top notch performances from the whole band; easily the album's highlight, and an obvious single (it eventually reached No 9). On a mellower note, 'Jealousy' and 'In Only Seven Days' fulfil the ballad quotient, while Brian's 'Leaving Home Ain't Easy' is arguably his finest self-sung track to date.

The album's release with a gatefold poster of the bicycle racers offended whole countries; added to that the music press's increasingly predictable opinions, initial forecasts were bleak. But despite *NME* accusing them of sounding like "third rate Gilbert and Sullivan" and advising "if you have a deaf relative, buy them this for Christmas", *Jazz* was soon nestling very comfortably at No 2 in the UK charts as it began its six month run.

Things were just as successful in America. With the album's inserted poster already banned there, the band were advised to play safe for the remainder of the tour. Their response? Have three naked women cycle onto the stage at Madison Square Garden, of course! That outing concluded in memorable style, the band returned home briefly before embarking on another European tour at the start of 1979. It was totally the norm by now, but yet again the amazing audience response everywhere was

overwhelming (beaten only by the next leg's mad whiz round their adoptive home, Japan).

Queen responded by playing better and better each night – just as well, because each European show was recorded for a possible live album release. With the decision taken to go ahead, the awesome task of actually wading through the tapes was begun, once again at Montreux's Mountain studios. In many ways the studios' superb views was one of the main reasons the band were able to square up to the daunting task ahead of them; in fact they enjoyed the place so much that, with typical aplomb, they bought it, lock, stock and barrel (rather than settle a frightening tax bill). When resident engineer David Richards dared to ask what Queen intended doing to his workplace, Fred's response might not have assured him: "Throw it in the lake, dear. What do you think?"

Work done, the results were publicly aired on 22 June 1979 under the title *Live Killers*. A double LP set, it captured the very heart of a Queen show and, for once, reviewers were pleased. Perhaps Sounds had to force themselves to admit it was "a perfectly adequate retrospective on most of their best songs", but *Record Mirror* were more gushing: "This is a triumph. Listen and you'll not be disappointed."

Strangely the fiercest criticism came from within the band, in particular from Roger who has since publicly disowned the album. But while it is a rough affair compared to the precise artistry of the studio works, the result is undeniably Queen live (only the merest cosmetic touches had been applied during production). For the first time on record the band's famed 'medley' is presented, this time including cracking versions of 'I'm In Love With My Car' and 'Bicycle Race'. The acoustic section is also wheeled out, featuring Freddie on "maracas and sometimes vocals" during a fine rendition of '39'. The perennially talked about 'Bohemian Rhapsody' doesn't fail to excite either, with its controversial taped middle section included before the band return

Main picture (right):

Fred's unique microphone technique came about by accident during a gig at the Wade Deacon Grammar School For Girls when his tall mike stand snapped. Not put off, he struggled on with it that night and for the next 20 years

to play out its heavy metal conclusion.

While the album hit No 3 in Britain, one of its finest components, the beautiful 'Love Of My Life', managed only No 63 when plucked as a single, while in America, the fast version of 'We Will Rock You' failed even to chart. Brian is fairly phlegmatic about the very notion of live albums: "Everyone tells you you have to do them and when you do you find that they're very often not of mass appeal, and in the absence of a fluke condition you sell your live album to the converted, the people who already know your stuff and come to the concerts. So if you add up the number of people who've come to see you over the last few years, that's very roughly the number who'll buy the live album, unless you have a hit single on it – which we didn't."

Whatever the thinking behind it, *Live Killers* maintained Queen's chart presence that year, leaving them free to concentrate on recording not one, but two new albums.

1979 was a strange year for Queen. *Live Killers* kept the band on people's turntables while a headlining slot at a major outdoor festival in Saarbrucken, Germany showed that the record wasn't a fluke. In between time, they spent the summer locked in Musicland studios in Munich working on albums 8 and 9 consecutively.

The first fruits of the sessions made a less than orthodox début. On 7 October, after weeks of practice, Freddie finally got to enact a personal dream: to appear in a ballet. He had already been thinking of wearing ballet shoes as part of a leather ensemble on stage, but now was the opportunity he had dreamed of. As part of a charity performance, Royal Ballet star Wayne Eagling invited Freddie to take part in a specially choreographed piece. When the day arrived, astounded audiences applauded as the Queen singer pranced his way through well rehearsed interpretations of 'Bohemian Rhapsody' and a new song, apparently called 'Crazy Little Thing Called Love'. While the reaction to 'Bo Rap' was ecstatic, Freddie was disappointed at the mute response to his new track – he forgot it was brand new and nobody knew it!

Within no time fans fell in love with the new song's open rockabilly innocence. Freddie had done it again! Elvis style lead and 50s pastiche backing combined with sparse period production and a gorgeous solo from Brian, uncustomarily playing a Fender Telecaster through a Boogie amp, all melded into one of the most distinctive sounds of the year. Not bad for a song Freddie wrote in a bubble bath in Germany!

The record immediately stormed to No 2 (their fourth time) and even the critics were pleased: "It's slick, smooth, fingersnapping and Freddie's voice suits it down to the ground," sang *Record Mirror*. In the States Elektra initially resisted calls for it to be released, but after import copies began filtering onto radio stations they knew they could delay no longer. In February 1980 it reached No 1. Everyone loved it.

The band took the success in their stride. Brian: "We're not a singles group, we don't stake our reputation on singles and we never have done, but I think it's brought a lot of younger people to our concerts." Perhaps it wasn't that important to the group, but it meant something special to one fan, as Roger remembers:

"I read somewhere – in Rolling Stone I think it was – that John Lennon heard it and it gave him the impetus to start recording again."

November 79 saw yet another tour undertaken, once again round Britain, but this time with a difference. Smaller venues was the name of the game, with the emphasis falling on Queen to reach the fans rather than have them swarm around the band. It was a nice idea, but first some seriously large venues were felt appropriate to satisfy the hard core. At the Birmingham NEC, in fact, Queen chalked up the record for highest indoor attendance with 14,000 fans. Another first for the tour was the sight of Freddie playing guitar on Crazy Little Thing. Brian didn't have to worry about his territory being invaded as Freddie claimed his guitar only knew three chords. "I've made no effort to become a guitar hero because I can't play the fucking guitar!" he later admitted.

The tour also saw the premiere of Queen's next single, the powerful ballad 'Save Me', featuring Brian on piano on stage (he had previously played piano on 'Teo Torriatte' in Japan). It went down well, as did the tour as a whole. After the larger halls were polished off, phase two of the tour swung into action: the so-called Crazy Tour. The next stage involved venues chosen for their intimacy rather than capacity; thus the Mayfair in Tottenham, the Rainbow Theatre and Tiffany's in Purley all found themselves playing host to just about the biggest band of the time – crazy indeed!

Although the tour had finished, Queen still found time for one more gig, at the behest of Paul McCartney who was putting together a charity concert to raise money for the starving in Kampuchea. They agreed to perform and on Boxing Day recorded a full concert from which 'Now I'm Here' was appropriated for the forthcoming charity album. 'Save Me' was released as a single in the UK on 25 January 1980, but the album remained unfinished for several months. Freddie

Main picture (right): **1984's Works Tour saw Queen play a controversial stint at South Africa's infamous Sun City, for which they were fined by the Musicians Union in England**

Picture (left): **The classic pose from the classic player. Brian gives 1984 audiences 'the works'**

PLAY THE GAME

took time out to buy a house in Kensington while on one of his rare visits to England; he also found time to record an hilarious piece for Kenny Everett's television show. Roger, meanwhile, hopped back over to Mountain to produce an act called Hilary Hilary, then home as Dominique did some producing of her own – their first child, Felix Luther.

With the album near completion, its first single proper was released. 'Play The Game' was Queen's 16th single, and the first Queen track to feature synthesisers; its video also saw Freddie unveiling his new image: the cropped hair and bushy moustache known throughout gay circles as the 'clone' look. Fans were aghast and sent razors to the band's offices; some even pelted him later on stage. The moustache question provided a welcome distraction, but in the end the press noticed the single – and hated it. "Indulgent, over produced trivia" was the *NME*'s view.

On its 30 June release the new album fared a little better – not from the *NME* of course who called *The Game* "old and tired and bland and blinkered" – with *Sounds* declaring "this is a straight kick into goal". Chart-wise, it shot to the top spot on both sides on the Atlantic as Queen set out on a new American tour. Standout tracks included all the singles plus a touching piano song from Brian, 'Sail Away Sweet Sister' and Roger's blood rousing 'Rock It'. But perhaps the most famous track on the album, certainly the best selling, came from John. Loosely shaped around a bass riff from Chic's 'Good Times', he crafted the most unlikely Queen hit to date, finally pushing the band out of their rock pigeon hole. "I listened to a lot of soul music when I was in school and I've always been interested in that sort of music," he recalls. "I'd been wanting to do a track like 'Another One Bites The Dust' for a while, but originally all I had was the line and the bass riff."

In America, black stations started picking up on the song; when ardent fan Michael Jackson suggested they release it, there was no argument. Within weeks Queen had another US No 1, only this time across the board, in the rock, disco and black soul charts, accumulating three million sales as they went. In the UK the song managed a relatively disappointing No 7 – but then it was the fourth single from the album.

The American tour rounded off with four nights at Madison Square Garden. Then it was back into the studios, this time in London's Anvil, to complete another project. Film producer Dino DeLaurentiis was putting together a remake of the 30s comic book adventure Flash Gordon; Queen were asked to do the soundtrack. Other bands had contributed to films before, but this was the first time a rock band had performed the whole score, as Brian recalls: "We saw 20 minutes of the finished film and thought it was very good and over the top. We'd been offered a few in the past, but most of them were where the film is written around music, and that's been done to death." In the end, the band sat and recorded their music like an old fashioned orchestra scoring a movie, watching the footage and as the gesture was made on screen, they responded.

Recording finished in November, but before anything was released there was the little matter of another European tour. It was not without controversy, however, due to Freddie's latest gimmick of being borne onto the stage by a costumed hunk. Superman was fine, but when a Darth Vader started appearing, its copyright owner George Lucas initiated legal proceedings to stop it (perhaps he was still smarting from Freddie's line "I don't like Star Wars" in Bicycle Race!).

On 24 November 1980, a new single, 'Flash', was released. Written by Brian it was a simple piece, made interesting by the various bits of dialogue intercut with the lyrics. The single reached No 10, as did its parent album, *Flash Gordon*. This was indeed a proper soundtrack, with only two vocal pieces. Fortunately the press received it as such and reaction was good: "Something extraordinary" said Sounds; "an album of truly epic proportions" was *Record Mirror's* verdict.

The album hit the shops on 8 December, just as the British leg was winding down at Wembley Arena, and the same night that Mark David Chapman pulled the trigger on John Lennon outside his New York home. Queen were devastated by the tragedy and during their show the next night, played a moving version of 'Imagine'.

The end of the decade fast approaching, the benefits of the tax exile began to show, with profits on *Jazz* and *Live Killers* coming in virtually untaxed, earning the band a place in the Guinness Book Of Records as the highest paid company directors in the country. On top of that it was announced that they had sold a mammoth 45 million albums and another 25 million singles worldwide in their first six years of success. If only they could carry their success into the next decade.

Main picture (left): "I like to ridicule myself. I don't take myself too seriously. I wouldn't wear these clothes if I was serious"
Insert: Freddie's outrageous female garb for 'I Want To Break Free' sparked a riot at 1985's Rock In Rio festival. This more innocuous outfit for 'It's A Hard Life' spared him the bottle treatment

To break themselves into the new decade and its incumbent challenges, Queen returned to Japan for five sell-out nights at the renowned Budokan Hall. The response of the Japanese fans was again phenomenal, on stage and off; Freddie was given the freedom of Tokyo's top store when it opened specially for him and Queen topped all the polls in Music Life.

With the certainty under their belts, it was now time for a trip into the unknown. Breaking new territories was something Queen were always keen to do, but since the mid 70s they had been running out of new audiences. Now they had one in their sights: South America. No other major act had made the trek so it was a huge investment, especially considering the rife corruption at all levels there, and the widespread poverty. But after nine months of planning and at a daily running cost of $25,000, the band began their most adventurous tour to date.

As the first stars to have paid any attention to the culture starved sub continent, Queen were accorded real royal status to fit their name. State police forces were at their beck and call, and everywhere they went, public dignitaries fell over themselves to shake their hands. The band's touchdown at Buenos Aires airport on 23 February was televised live, proving Queen were the biggest stars there since Eva Peron. The actual business of making music was not overlooked, however, and despite the band's fears about the language barrier, the opening shows proved the audiences to be just the same as anywhere else in the world. Freddie in particular felt enormous relief: "We were really nervous. We had no right to automatically expect the works from an alien territory." They needn't have feared; each show was a sell-out. At Morumbi Stadium in São Paulo they broke the world record for a paying audience when they played in front of 131,000 ecstatic fans. Only their live broadcast around Brazil and Argentina reached a larger number of people (35 million to be precise!).

Without question, the South American experience had been a success, whetting the band's appetites for further foreign adventure. Roger: "I wouldn't mind playing Russia at some time. But over there you have to be carefully vetted by the government.

The Russian authorities like Cliff Richard and Elton John, but Queen are still considered a little bit wild."

Closer to home, Roger realised another ambition with the release of his second solo single and first solo album, *Fun In Space*. Future Management's synthesised chorus contrasted deeply with the balladic simplicity of the B-side 'Laugh Or Cry', but the effect as a whole was generally one of cohesion. *Sounds* amusingly praised his "laudable attempt to step out of the shadow of the toothy one" and he had some success. The single only reached No 49, although the LP made it up to 16 – far better than the US single, 'Let's Get Crazy', or the UK's follow-up, 'My Country' which both failed to chart. It was the first bona fide attempt by a member of the group to exist outside Queen and it provoked many fears that the band were on the verge of splitting – everyone knew they were more colleagues than close friends these days and feared the worst. But it never came to that. Queen was their lives; it had cost them too much to get where they were to throw it away now.

Brian also had a new release of sorts with the birth of his second child, Louisa, on 22 May 1981. He managed to be around for the birth, but then had to answer the call of the studio and fly out to Montreux for work on the next studio album. With no marriage imminent (or ever likely – his relationship with Mary had become more platonic as he realised his natural homosexual desires) Freddie's time and money were spent on close friends, never more so than for his birthday. That year he flew all his dearest chums to New York on Concorde for a party that was to last five days in a typical show of excess.

Not long after, the band returned to South America, fittingly calling it the Gluttons For Punishment Tour, to play in Venezuela and Mexico. The audiences yet again were a revelation, but external forces ruined the visit. Shows were cancelled left, right and centre for various reasons. The death of the Venezuelan President didn't help as an enforced period of national mourning saw more gigs forsaken; after only two shows in Mexico they realised they might never get paid and scrapped the rest of the tour and ran home for cover.

Main picture (left):

The Magic Tour played to 1,000,000 people over 26 dates, grossing £11,000,000

A little battle scarred, but unharmed, 26 October saw a very special Queen release. During recording sessions at Mountain, one of the local residents had wandered up for a look around. His name was David Bowie, and in almost fairytale fashion, he didn't leave that day until the bones and a lot of the flesh of a new song had been created (he also contributed some fine BVs to a song called 'Cool Cat' – check bootlegs for confirmation). Fred, Roger and Bowie later buffed the track into shape and 'Under Pressure' became Queen's second No 1 (after four near misses). While Queen were thrilled with the result (Roger: "It's one of the very best things Queen have ever done") and added it to their set instantly, Bowie was less impressed and rarely played it before his appearance at the Freddie Mercury Tribute Concert in 1992. "It sort of half came off but I think it could have been a lot better," he later said.

As is the custom, an album was released soon after, on 7 November. Strangely, in this case it didn't feature the chart topping single of the moment (not in the UK anyway; in other territories it did), largely because it had been prepared to run almost a year earlier but was held over when *Flash Gordon* kept on selling. That song aside, *Greatest Hits* was the name, and *Greatest Hits* most certainly was its game. Seventeen classic tracks stood side by side to provide the perfect aural tribute to the band's first 10 years together. To help the celebrations, a collection of videos (Greatest Flix) and a book (Greatest Pix) were also released; each item leapt to the top of its respective charts.

As the summary of their careers so far, *Greatest Hits* was an impressive package, and has since become the best selling album in the UK. Not bad for a group who weren't supposed to be a 'singles band'...

Main picture:

"We're the Cecil B De Mille of rock. Always trying to do things bigger and better" – Freddie

In no time at all Queen's *Greatest Hits* was sitting at the top of the charts, but for the celebration to be complete, they needed some account of their live prowess – that was what they prided themselves on after all. So it was that they played two sold-out nights in Montreal, Canada to a total of 36,000 people. That city's film company MobileVision filmed both nights with a view to releasing the finished work as a sort of Queen tour by proxy: the film would travel around the world to places where Queen were unlikely to visit and be played on huge outdoor screens to create as much of a real concert atmosphere as possible. That was the idea; in reality it failed to meet its deadline, and financial arguments made it a project soonest forgotten.

Main picture (right): **In 1993 Brian embarked on a world tour in support of his** Back To The Light **album. The show at London's Brixton Academy was recorded for future release**

Picture (above): **"Bar-ce-looo-naa!"**

From Montreal to Munich, Queen's adoptive home. While Montreux was a great place to work, Fred in particular revelled in the inner city hubbub he got from the German studio, preferring it to the picturesque milieu of Switzerland's sleepy resort. He also found it easier to stroll down streets undisturbed than he did in London; and his 'clone' look fitted in perfectly. But the city held an allure for everyone, according to Brian: "Munich had a huge effect on all our lives. Because we spent so much time there it became almost another home and a place in which we lived different lives. In retrospect it's probably true to say that our efficiency in Munich was not very good. Our social habits made us generally start work late in the day, feeling tired, and for me especially, and perhaps for Freddie, the emotional distractions became destructive."

No matter; after the world shattering success of *The Game*, it obviously had its benefits as well. As recording took them into the new year, they were joined in Munich by the American star Billy Squier. They soon became good friends, so much so that Freddie and Roger found themselves in the wrong studio one day putting down backing vocals on his track 'Emotions In Motion' when they should have been working next door on their own record. With his taste for 'guesting' whetted, Roger was soon contributing drums to Gary Numan's *Dance* album back in London (he played on three tracks: 'Crash', 'Morals' and 'You Are You Are').

Studio work completed, there was still, naturally, another tour. This time the lucky audience was Europe with the first gig taking place at Gothenburg's Scandinavium on 8 April. Things were a little different this time around; the light show wasn't quite as dominating as before (and it didn't have a silly name!), and the support act, Bow Wow Wow, were felt by audiences to be inappropriate and were subsequently chided into abandoning the tour – a rare feat. But the most significant alteration was made within the group: with synthesisers now increasingly part of their live norm (they had made their first appearance on the last tour), neither Freddie nor Brian could spare the time to play them, so a fifth limb was added to the touring beast in the shape of Mott The Hoople's colourful keyboard ace, Morgan Fisher.

On 1 April the band renewed their contract with EMI, this time committing themselves to a further six albums. The first example of work under the new contract came 18 days later with the appearance of a rather risqué looking single sleeve featuring close ups of a naked couple, clothed only in paint. The song, fittingly, was called Body Language, and the wild images didn't stop there. The video, directed by Mike Hodges, featured a troupe of daubed performers writhing around a steamy set, while the band very

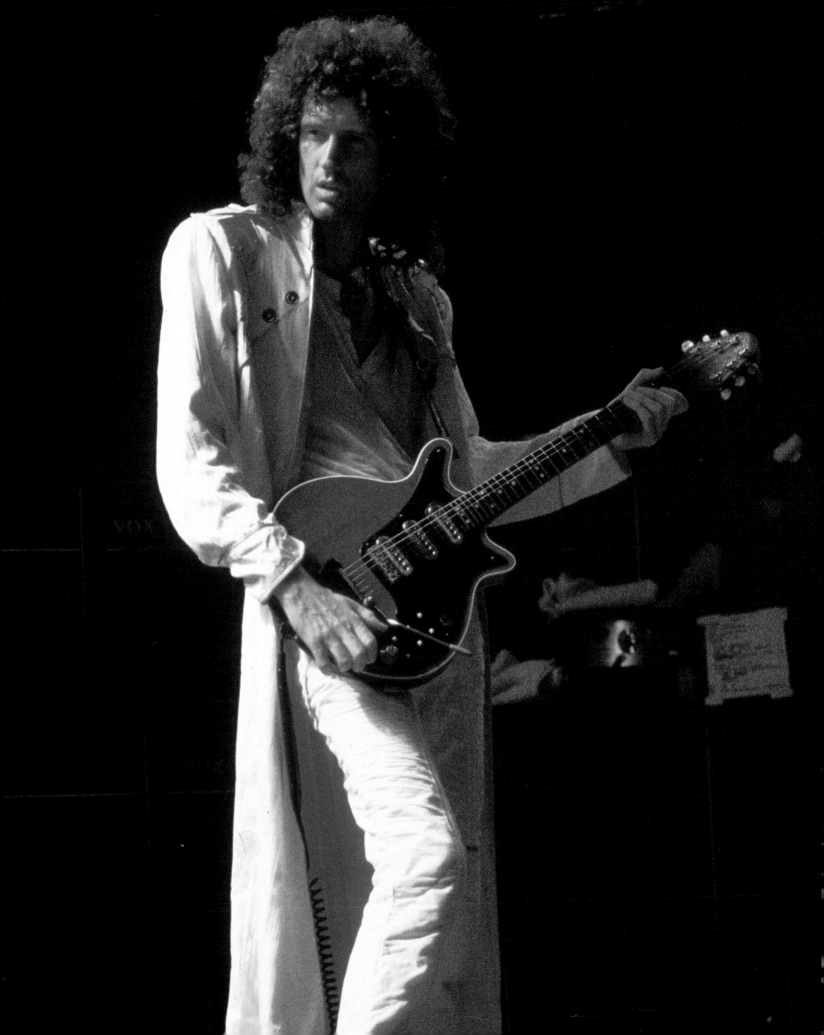

obviously remained fully clothed (and rather hot looking). Unfortunately, most people never got to see the results as the video was banned by MTV and other stations. In America the sleeve itself had to be swapped for a more discreet plain cover.

In the resulting furore the music was almost forgotten; for many fans that wouldn't have been a bad thing, as hordes registered their dissatisfaction with the band's pro funk leanings. But you can't offend all of the people all of the time, and to prove that *Sounds* were quite glowing: "Good, electronically pulsed cooled out slick 133 BPM 7" white disco smash." It didn't help the song get any higher than a poor 25, 18 in America.

At the same time the band were being largely ignored by the record buying public in their own hemisphere, they were inadvertently reaping the rewards of the previous year's frontier breaking ventures. During their tour of South America, all Queen's albums sat in the various national Top 10s there, while 'Love Of My Life' spent a year in the charts before departing, so obviously they had a keen following who liked them on record as well as live. In April 1982 then, it should have been no surprise when 'Under Pressure' hit No 1 in Argentina; but it was a remarkable achievement, due to the fact that Britain was currently at war with Argentina over the group of islands called the Falklands/Malvinas. Given his cosmopolitan upbringing, Freddie was typically dismissive of the debate: "It's our young men killing their young men. There's no glory in being blown to bits." The Argentine government weren't so magnanimous and banned all Queen records and forbade them from playing there again.

On 21 May *Hot Space* was finally sent out to face the public's wrath. The addition of synths was certainly noted, with many critics pointing to their inclusion as the reason for the album's weakness. But it wasn't as cut and dry as that; 'Put Out The Fire', 'Dancer' and 'Action This Day' are as heavy as other Queen songs, and of course there's the marvellous 'Under Pressure' holding up the rear so things can't have been that bad. Unfortunately as soon as people heard the opening track 'Staying Power', complete with "hot and spacey horns" from Arif Mardin, John's funk by numbers 'Back Chat' and the listless 'Cool Cat', they dismissed the whole album as second rate disco. At the time, Brian was defensive of the album, saying "it was an attempt to do funk properly". Hindsight hasn't altered his opinion, but he now understands the problem. "I think *Hot Space* was a mistake, if only timing-wise," he recalls. "We got heavily into funk and it was quite similar to what Michael Jackson did on *Thriller* a couple of years later and the timing was wrong. Disco was a dirty word."

As the tour reached Britain Freddie made his opinions on the

reactions known. "It's only a bloody record!" he ticked off the crowd at Milton Keynes and, due to the fact the show was being recorded for TV broadcast as part of The Tube, he was effectively telling the world. Strangely, reviews for *Hot Space* were some of the best Queen had ever had. "New styles and a whole new sense of values" – *Record Mirror*; "*Hot Space* shows more restraint and imagination than tripe like *Jazz* – *Sounds*; "the production of the whole album is really a peach" – *NME*. It eventually chalked up a No 4 position in the UK which wasn't bad, and 22 in the States, which was.

The main worry, especially in America, was that Queen had lost their rock roots. This was not the case, as witnesses to their European tour can testify. Leeds' Elland Road stadium hosted a supercharged band who rocked harder than the city had ever seen. At Milton Keynes they even managed to make the funk work for the crowds, as Brian remembers: " 'Staying Power', especially, sounds even tighter than the record, and heavier."

Two more singles attempted to keep Queen alive in the UK – Brian's Spanish flavoured ballad 'Las Palabras De Amor (The Words Of Love)' and 'Back Chat', reaching Nos 17 and 40 respectively – and then it was time to try and repair the damage Stateside. It wasn't easy, and the single released there, Roger's 'Calling All Girls' (incidentally his first A-side anywhere!) didn't help after flagging at No 60. But it was not all doom and gloom. Once attracted into the theatres, audiences were as enthusiastic as ever and gradually some ground was clawed back. In Boston a 'Queen Day' was declared in their honour. "They were all so enthusiastic," Brian recalls, "they had parades and Queen events. It was great, they loved us." If any further proof were needed that as a live phenomenon Queen were unrivalled, their annual sell-out at Madison Square Garden pretty much wrapped it up. But the recorded arena remained a problem, as 'Staying Power' was released to absolutely no chart success. If the band could still pack stadiums throughout America, then the fault had to lie elsewhere; Elektra were dropped as Queen's record company in the US.

Main picture (left):

"Our new show will have more light and spectacle than the Vatican" – Roger

Insert:

"We have gotten to the stage in our lives where we don't tour very much. We are working less as a group these days than as four individuals" – John

LIFE IS REAL

The group's newly chosen label, Capitol, were rightly delighted at having Queen on side. Unfortunately, 1983 would be the first year in their careers when the band didn't release an album. They didn't even tour. For the first time in their lives they took real time off, from work and, more importantly, from each other.

"We were getting too close to each other," Brian now admits, "getting on each other's nerves, which happens periodically. This time we said, Let's take a break and give ourselves some breathing space. Let's do individual things then we can come back to Queen when we actually feel motivated. We took about five months off work. During this time we met and talked a lot but we didn't actually do anything."

Roger puts the sabbatical on another footing: "After touring America, Europe and Japan we were totally knackered, so we thought we deserved a bit of a rest. It also had a lot to do with the last album not doing as well as previous LPs. We realised that it hadn't been what a lot of fans wanted or expected from us so we

thought a break would give us the opportunity to think things through a bit."

Inevitably the press perceived the rest as a split, but that was never going to be the case. Queen had come to mean too much to everyone; and regardless of internal wranglings, what would they do without it? "None of us has any intention of leaving," Freddie stressed at the time. "It would be cowardice to stop now. The chemistry has worked for us, so why kill the goose that lays the golden egg?" There was another, equally practical reason for not quitting: "It's got to the point where we're all actually too old to break up. Can you imagine forming a new band at 40? Be a bit silly, wouldn't it?"

For whatever reason, the 10th anniversary year of Queen's first album saw them release... absolutely nothing. The landmark passed by without a record or a concert.

But while things may have been quiet on the group front, each individual member remained far from indolent with solo activities busying them up to the hilt. Freddie kicked things off with some work on his long suggested solo album. More than any other member, he was the one people expected to branch out on his own; now he was getting the chance. There was only one place he would even consider recording, and within no time he was back at Musicland in the heart of his beloved Munich. Work was fast, but results were slow coming – without the others there to act as his customary sounding board, Fred's own strive for perfection ran away with him. As a further delay, synthesiser supremo Georgio Moroder approached him with a view to contributing to a new soundtrack for Fritz Lang's silent classic film, Metropolis. Enthused by the challenge, Freddie threw himself into the project, even though the result, 'Love Kills', would not make it onto his own album.

On top of that, he also hooked up with Michael Jackson in New York and together they worked on several ideas. What exactly was produced during this time is a matter of some speculation. In 1993 the Queen office denied the existence of any material, but Freddie himself has said that three tracks were worked on: one of

Main picture:

When Freddie's 'clone' look first appeared fans threw razors onto the stage and posted them to his house

Picture (left):

"I certainly don't have any aspirations to live to 70. It would be boring" – Freddie (1987)

Michael's, one of his, and one they co-wrote. Of the three, Michael's 'State Of Shock' turned up on a Jacksons album with Mick Jagger and not Freddie dueting the lead. Freddie: "Michael called me and said could I come over and finish the song there and then, but I couldn't make it at that time, he couldn't wait, and so suddenly it was released without me on it." Of the remaining pair there is no record, although Freddie did say that the song they co-wrote was called 'Victory' – the name given by Michael to the next Jacksons album.

Roger was also active, both solo, and with collaborations. A skiing break was punctuated by stops at Mountain to lay down some ideas he had for his next solo effort. On one visit, Status Quo's Rick Parfitt accompanied him and ended up co-writing one track, while John Deacon played bass on another. John's own solo efforts were somewhat hindered by his inability to sing, but that didn't stop him laying down some bass lines for 'Man Friday And Jive Junior's Picking Up Sounds' and jamming with a host of pop chums, among them tennis stars Vitas Gerulaitis and John McEnroe. That aside, 1983 for him was pretty much a family time – hard work in itself considering the size of his family (his fourth child, Joshua, arrived in December).

That just left Brian. Buying the Red Special its own aeroplane seat (he wouldn't trust the luggage hold with something that valuable), he set off for Los Angeles where he played on two tracks by Jeffrey Osborne 'Stay With Me Tonight' and 'Two Wrongs Don't Make A Right' before tying up with some very special friends for a unique jamming session. Edward Van Halen, Fred Mandel, Reo Speedwagon's Alan Gratzer and Phil Chen from the Rod Stewart band all joined Brian at the Record Plant for a day of extemporised playing. They worked on three tracks: the theme to one of Jimmy May's favourite shows, 'Star Fleet', an old song of Brian's, 'Let Me Out', plus a freewheeling made-up-as-they-went-along-all-out-jam (later christened 'Bluesbreaker'). Everyone played brilliantly, especially EVH on the last track, but nothing was planned for the finished versions. Just in case, though, Brian got everyone's permission to tinker with the results and see what came up.

Back in London, Brian was approached to produce a young Scottish band called Heavy Pettin', a task he was initially wary of committing himself to, having produced no one but Queen for the last decade. But with the trusty Rheinhardt Mack at his side completing the partnership that had produced Flash Gordon (the rest of the band made do with 'Executive Producer' tags on that occasion), he threw himself into it, notching up the first of many such extra-Queen dalliances to come. (Mack also co-produced with Queen The Game and Hot Space.)

With so many outside interests consuming everyone's time, it came as no surprise that the only thing to get them all together was talk of another project – another soundtrack. Jim Beach had become involved in the filming of John Irving's new book Hotel New Hampshire, to star Rob Lowe and Jodie Foster, and wanted the band to do the soundtrack. After a meeting with the director Tony Richardson, Freddie and John recommended to the rest of the group that they go ahead with it. After the backlash against the last album, this sounded like it could be fun.

Suitably inspired, the whole band convened in August to run through some ideas. As a unit they'd had too many bad experiences at the European studios so decided that a change of scenery could help smooth relations. Brian had enjoyed his brief spell at the Record Plant and the whole band liked the idea of working in Los Angeles, and so it was to California they headed to record for the first time in their careers.

It didn't take long for them to realise that the soundtrack was not going to materialise. Once the decision was made, they were then free to concentrate all efforts on a proper album. Work lasted into the new year, frustrating Queen fans and record companies alike. Some partial appeasement came to both parties with the release of a mini album from Brian on 31 October: Star Fleet Project. The finished article made no claim to be a polished work of art, although Brian had tidied it up a bit in the studio. It was basically the sounds of five master musicians having a blast, and it shows. Some of the ad libs left in are better than many scripted licks, and even the title track (complete with some extra help from Roger on the choruses) goes way beyond the limits of what is basically a twee theme tune thanks to some outstanding playing. A single edit of 'Star Fleet' peaked at No 65 and the mini album reached 35 in the UK. It made a decent diversion, but for Queen fans the next major event wouldn't arrive for another three months.

Main picture:

"If something's worth doing, it's worth overdoing"

But for a few slight alterations, concert crowds in their thousands could have very easily been asked to chant something quite different from the classic refrain they so quickly warmed to. Inspired by the infantile mutterings of his son Felix, Roger Taylor structured a pop classic. "Felix came out with 'Radio Poo Poo', I thought that sounded good, so I changed it around a bit and came up with 'Radio Ga Ga'," Roger remembers. "The song came after I locked myself in a studio for three days with a synthesiser and a drum machine." From Radio Poo Poo to Radio Ka Ka to its present name, Taylor's song provided the springboard needed to launch Queen's mid 80s resurgence after the muted success of *Hot Space*.

For all its assured swagger, 'Radio Ga Ga' was actually Roger's first world-wide A-side single release (although 'Calling All Girls' had been aired in the States). It was never the case that his songs were weaker than the others' – or they would never have made the album – but more likely due to his insistence on singing most of his own compositions; however good the song, no record company would accept a single that ignored Queen's strongest trait: Fred's voice.

'Radio Ga Ga' was released on 23 January 1984 to reviews ranging from "masterly pop construction" (*Smash Hits*) to "arrogant nonsense" (*NME*, natch). As ever the public voted with their wallets and it vaulted into the UK charts at No 4, equalling the eight year record of 'Somebody To Love'. Unfortunately, like STL, after its superlative start momentum was lost and it had to settle for an eventual runner-up position behind Frankie Goes To Hollywood's controversial 'Relax'. The UK notwithstanding, the song went on to top the charts in 19 countries, thanks in no small part to its stunning video from director David Mallett featuring an army of clapping fan club members, Freddie and the boys in leather trousers and footage from Metropolis, on loan from the German government! (Ironically, despite the success of the video the song is an attack on the power of MTV and suchlike in the 80s record scene.) The song was further made special by its non album B-side, the raucous (and quite funny) 'I Go Crazy'; it was also the first record to feature a personalised catalogue number from EMI – QUEEN 1.

In America 'Ga Ga' climbed to 16, not bad but disappointing given it was Capitol's first chance to prove themselves. Its parent album, *The Works*, came out first in the States (24 February), peaking at No 23 – hardly the volte face sales-wise they'd hoped for, as Brian admits: "In spite of the enthusiastic start with the new company, *The Works* did, if anything, worse than *Hot Space* overall in the USA."

Back home things were quite different. Released on 27 February *The Works* shot straight to No 2 where it remained, seemingly forever, behind the record breaking *Legend* album by Bob Marley which gripped the top slot for 12 weeks. With cover shots by famed Hollywood photographer George Hurrell, it certainly looked the business, and the band were more than happy with it sounds-wise. "It's going to be called *The Works* and it really is!" Brian enthused on its release. "There's all the Queen trademarks. Lots of production, arrangements and harmonies." After the focusing on one style on *Hot Space*, the new album took in a broader array of influences. 'Crazy Little Thing Called Love Part II' arrived courtesy of Fred's 'Man On The Prowl', while Roger and Brian, in an unusual co-writing situation, explored the computer age with 'Machines (Or Back To Humans)'. Arguably the catchiest track was the one that started the project, one of the first ideas laid down for possible inclusion in the Hotel New

Hampshire soundtrack; 'Keep Passing The Open Windows' is actually a recurring line in the book intended to keep spirits up; in retrospect it is arguably Freddie's last great song of the 80s.

For what it was worth, most of the press found the album a pleasant experience. *Sounds* were especially moved by the "excellent 'Hammer To Fall'", while *Record Mirror* claimed the whole package was "another jewel in the crown". *Smash Hits* admitted the album's sweeping range of song styles to be a bold move but concluded, 'Keep Passing The Open Windows' aside, "none of them are really any good". In the end, the battle was fought as usual in the record stores, and soon *The Works* had become second only to *Greatest Hits* in terms of units shifted.

The album's success was obviously a result of many things, not least the band's continued presence in the singles charts. Next cab off the ranks was John Deacon's 'I Want To Break Free', now slightly longer than the album version thanks to the inclusion of several synth passages. The song threw up a couple of anomalies: on a musical note, one reviewer likened Brian's guitar solo to the sounds more likely to emanate from "Sweep, the celebrated glove puppet", when actually Brian never played the solo; he admits it was sessioneer Fred Mandel on keyboards. Secondly, the accompanying video sees the band sending up Britain's longest running soap opera, *Coronation Street*, with all four of them in drag. For reasons known only to himself, Freddie refused to shave off his moustache for his portrayal of the vacuuming vamp – fair enough, you might think, but then for the middle section based on Debussy's ballet 'L'Après-Midi D'un Faune', he unfathomably appeared sans said facial hirsuteness.

The song had mixed fortunes. In the UK it reached No 3 and became one of the band's best selling tracks, largely because of the hilarious video. In the USA it singlehandedly killed off Queen as a major rock act – Americans failed to see beyond the dresses. Perhaps not unsurprisingly, Freddie received a lot of the blame for the cross dressing stunt, but at the time he denied the accusation. "The idea actually came from Roger," he revealed. "Actually the others ran into their frocks quicker than anything."

Promotion for the album took various guises. Roger and John embarked on a marathon press session, seeing off 112 interviews between them in 16 days! Then there was the band's visit to the San Remo Music Festival in Italy – basically a huge version of Top Of The Pops where they mimed their way valiantly through 'Radio Ga Ga' to outstanding applause; this was actually their first performance in the country. That done there was the similar matter of Switzerland's Golden Rose Pop Festival in Montreux, where lip syncing was again the order of the day, much to

everyone's annoyance. But it had to be done, as Roger admitted: "All events like this are farces 'cause you're miming to playback, but Freddie made that pretty obvious. But 400 million viewers – who could say no?"

Despite his loathing of the medium, Roger undertook further miming duties recording the video to his fourth solo single, 'Man On Fire'. Unfortunately it was largely a futile effort as the video was banned by MTV and other shows for featuring a burning building without showing a girl occupant escaping. The song's poor chart showing was arguably due to a sense of Queen fatigue in the public, and perhaps had it been released a year earlier the song would have climbed higher than 66. Certainly it was a good sales pitch for the album, *Strange Frontier*, itself a much stronger, more whole affair than *Fun In Space*. But despite the inclusion of Springsteen and Dylan covers and a song co-penned with Rick Parfitt, the album reached only No 30, and then for a brief stay. The title track was released as a single but fared even worse, despite an imaginative video that attempts to encapsulate James Dean's 'Rebel Without A Cause' in one four minute promo.

Brian meanwhile was working on a solo project with a difference. He had been having talks with US guitar manufacturers Guild about recreating his Red Special, and in June the first production line models of the BHM1 went on sale for £1,200. Brian was pleased with the result – at last he had a worthy backup for stage

work – until Guild attempted to market a budget version, at which point he withdrew his blessing.

Business for Queen continued as usual with single No 3 being plucked from the cosy confines of *The Works*. 'It's A Hard Life', Freddie's lavish ballad swept to No 6 in the UK, once again strongly supported by a lavish video. While Fred radiates enthusiasm from beneath his

Main picture (left): **Caught in the spotlight**

Picture (above): **Freddie's technique of crossing his hands during 'Bohemian Rhapsody' would horrify teachers – but it worked**

waist length black wig, the rest of the band look obviously ill at ease with the whole production. "I've tried to get most of my scenes cut," admitted Roger later.

With the Queen machine fully firing, there was only one thing missing from such a successful year: a tour. Needless to say, in the words of the song they got "Stickells to see to that" and were soon embarking on a lengthy European itinerary. This time around Spike Edney, ex-Boomtown Rats, handled second piano and synth duties, plus extra guitar in 'Hammer To Fall', and the backdrop was based extensively on Metropolis's scenery with a couple of huge cogs – the works, geddit? – thrown in. Brussels was the first city to experience the show, and there something happened that would come to typify Queen concerts. In 'Radio Ga Ga', every member of the crowd clapped their hands during the choruses to create a breathtaking sea of arms, moving together like corn in the wind. Just as well the audience was on top form that night, because they were actually being filmed as part of the video to the band's next single, Brian's anti armageddon 'Hammer To Fall'.

After the surprise reaction to 'Ga Ga' in Brussels, the good folk of Birmingham were given a chance to witness something unusual during the band's gigs at the *NEC*. As Spike struck up the synthesised intro to 'I Want To Break Free', crowds searched the stage for the lead singer. They didn't have to wait long – on he pranced wearing the video's regulation black wig and pink top while pushing his mike stand like a vacuum cleaner. But typically Freddie took the video one stage further and delighted one and all by sporting a mammoth pair of plastic breasts beneath his tight top; he then took great pleasure in exposing 'them' to the audience before apparently smothering John's face with same. Another first for Queen!

Another first for Freddie was the release of his first solo single which came out on the same day as 'Hammer To Fall'.' Love Kills', the song he co-wrote with Georgio Moroder, was a stark contrast to the Queen rocker, trading Queen's customary guitar orchestrations for synthesised approximations. But Freddie sang his socks off (although one reviewer said he sounded like the nasal Nik Kershaw!) and the song actually reached No 10 to HTF's 13 (no sign of the Queen fatigue suffered by Mr Taylor!).

In Germany the first setback occurred. During a particularly energetic rendition of 'Hammer To Fall', Freddie landed awkwardly, tearing the fragile ligaments he had injured earlier in the year during some night club high jinx. Roadies quickly ferried him off stage to administer what help they could, but it was no good, he couldn't go on. But never one to let the crowd down,

Freddie insisted on being carried to his piano from where the band rattled through 'Bo Rap' and 'Champions' before the anguished singer was whisked to hospital in Berlin.

With Fred back on stage two days later (strictly against doctors' orders!), his health held out until the European leg had finished before another ailment struck. The band had agreed to play a dozen shows at South Africa's legendary millionaires' playground, Sun City, flying in the face of public opinion once again, but just a couple of numbers into the first gig Fred's voice gave in and that show, plus the next four, had to be cancelled. It was hardly the most auspicious start, but it served them right according to many commentators who were peeved that Queen had agreed to play in a country that in 1984 still practised apartheid. Their very appearance was to dog them for years to come, but at the time they felt justified in their actions, after all, the shows were in front of mixed, non-segregated audiences. As Queen saw it, they were actually doing some good in a very small way. "We're totally against apartheid and all it stands for," Brian stated afterwards, "but I feel we did a lot of bridge building. We actually met musicians of both colours. They all welcomed us with open arms. The only criticism we got was from outside South Africa."

Politically, Queen alienated themselves from the rest of the world (a later single from Artists Against Apartheid, 'We're Not Gonna Play Sun City', was a direct attack on them), but success-wise it was just another unclaimed territory like South America, begging to be tamed. Unfortunately, Freddie's admission that "there's a lot of money to be made" in South Africa focused the criticism, perhaps unfairly considering that a large portion of Queen's earnings from the experience were given to various black charities in the country. They even released a South Africa only live album to pay for a new wing at the Kutlawamong School for blind and deaf children, but this was not enough according to the Musicians Union in the UK who fined the band for their visit and banned them from ever repeating the experience. Roger summed up the band's mood at the time: "In a way I do regret playing. In some ways I would defend what we did. I mean basically we play music to people – lots of them preferably – and I think a lot of crap is talked over here about things people don't really know about."

Determined to prove they still had a sense of humour after everything that had happened, the group went back into the studio (albeit separately) to work on an contrivedly upbeat new track. With more than a little sense of relief, Roger and Brian came up with a song called 'Thank God It's Christmas', obviously aimed at the Yuletide market. Released on 26 November it crept to No 21 in the UK, sparking little reaction from buyers and press alike. Richard Skinner on Whistle Test memorably paid a backhanded compliment to the band's efficiency: "This song was apparently written, recorded and produced in two days – and it sounds like it."

'Thank God It's Christmas' may not have set imaginations racing that winter, but for fans it offered a chance to buy a non-album track. It was the first single released that year not from *The Works*, although its B-sides – 'Man On The Prowl' and 'Keep Passing The Open Windows' – meant that every song from the album was available on a single somewhere (many of them in extended versions on 12" singles: 'Man On The Prowl', 'Keep Passing The Open Windows', 'Radio Ga Ga', 'I Want To Break Free', 'It's A Hard Life' and 'Hammer To Fall' were all to be found in lengthened forms).

As well as regurgitating all its content on the single format, *The Works* scored a rather more remarkable achievement. Of the four songs selected as A-sides, each is written by a different member – a feat unparalleled in popular music, even by The Beatles. The fact stands as testament to Queen's rich talent, but it also hints at a band keener on pleasing its shareholders than following its heart.

Single selection is a strange affair, of course, and the one thing which caused more arguments than any other in Queen. Sad though it is to admit, the problem had nothing to do with kudos, and everything to do with the extra royalties earned on 7" releases. Brian: "We always rowed about money. A lot of terrible injustices take place over songwriting. The major one is B-sides. Like, 'Bohemian Rhapsody' sells a million and Roger gets the same writing royalties as Freddie because he did 'I'm In Love With My Car'. There was contention about that for years."

Arguably the problem had arisen with Freddie a decade earlier as the band reworked the song 'Lover' into 'Liar' and he took sole writing credit on the grounds that he'd come up with the lyric. "It may not have been the most logical decision," Brian admits now, "but it was workable." What may have been the easy way out at the time soon had negative effects, however. "The rule almost certainly discouraged us from co-operating on lyrics for a long time, and started a trend towards separateness in song producing in general, which was acute at the time of the Munich records."

Within a few years Queen were to take a decision to eradicate all squabbles derived from royalties, but for now they edged their way forward as best they could, with Brian and Roger penning two songs between them in 84, and Freddie and Brian one other, while the next year they would come up with a single credited entirely to Queen. If the year's trials and accusations had taught them anything, it was that the group had to stick together.

Background picture:
Others emulated him but no one matched Freddie for charisma, poise or power

Picture (above):
The largest stage Wembley had ever seen is enough to tire even the fittest guitarist

Five Top 30 singles, a multi-platinum album and sell-out tour in Europe and South Africa plus awards by the sack load made 1984 a hard act to follow, but Queen were never ones to rest on their laurels. January saw their massive touring machine installing itself in Brazil for the world's largest rock festival, Rock In Rio. As South America's honorary sons Queen were given the prestigious privilege of topping the bill on both the opening and closing nights of the week long event.

The festival was held at the massive Barra da Tijuca in Rio, capable of holding a record 250,000 people. The other names on the bill would have been headliners any other time, but in South America the likes of Ozzy Osbourne, AC/DC, Iron Maiden and Def Leppard all had to wait in line behind Queen. Although they were top of the bill, when the band first stepped out on stage on 12 January, even they were surprised by the emotional welcome. Clearly a lot of friends from 1981 had turned up, but whoever they were, they were bowled over by the band's performance. Only one moment scarred things: when 'I Want To Break Free' kicked off and Fred appeared in his customary drag outfit, he was sensationally bottled and jeered. He quickly removed the offending 'falsies' and things continued as before. The band later learned the reason for the mysterious backlash was buried in the fact that the song had been adopted all over the country as a campaign anthem in the name of freedom; by performing it with massive mammaries strapped to his chest, Freddie was seen to denigrate the efforts of the liberation movement.

The rest of the festival passed without incident, just plenty of partying and myriad events held in the band's honour. Queen's next dates weren't until April in New Zealand and Australia, which left them time for other projects. Roger and Mountain man David Richards joined forces to produce various projects for Jimmy Nail, Sideway Look and Feargal Sharkey; Roger also appeared on Roger Daltrey's tribute to Who drummer Keith Moon, 'Under A Raging Moon'. Freddie, meanwhile, on a visit to the Heaven night club bumped into the man he would later call "my husband". Fellow clone dresser Jim Hutton was a hairdresser at the Savoy in London when he met the singer; after a rocky start (Fred told Jim to "Fuck off") the two became inseparable.

The antipodean tour underway in April, Freddie's solo career proper was launched with the release of the single 'I Was Born To Love You'. Poppier and more obviously synth based than anything Queen had ever done, it surprised a lot of people, eventually surging to No 11 in the charts. The album *Mr Bad Guy* followed on 29 April and achieved the same instant success as the single. Comparisons with Queen are to be expected, but a glance at how Fred's efforts stood up to Roger's solo dabblings is also worthwhile. Bearing in mind that one of the pair held an Art diploma and the other was a qualified dentist, it is all credit to Taylor that the sleeve for *Strange Frontier* is so well thought out and quite attractively put together; the cover of *Mr Bad Guy* on the other hand, consists of just a large mug shot of the man himself squinting into the sun.

On the musical side, again many pundits favour Taylor's album, suggesting that the only obstacle in the way of commercial success is the fact that Fred's voice is nowhere to be heard. For his part, Mercury stepped clearly out of Queen's shadow by turning in a collection of songs ranging from piano ballads to hi-NRG stompers, but all of them heavily marked by the influences of dance music. 'Man Made Paradise' features some prominent

guitar, but the majority of the tracks promote the abilities of the synthesiser, whether it be for taking the place of a whole orchestra (supposedly) or providing the furious

Main picture: **Cool cat**

Picture (above): **"I don't want to change the world with our music. I like to write songs for fun, for modern consumption. People can discard them like a used tissue afterwards" –** *Freddie*

rhythms. More than ever before, Fred was living his claim that his songs were "like Bic razors, for fun, for modern consumption. You listen to it, like it, discard it then on to the next. Disposable pop." Unsurprisingly, *Mr Bad Guy* is out and out fun, from start to finish, with each song sounding like a possible single. But whatever the style, they all have one theme. "I write commercial love songs because basically what I feel strongly about is love and emotion," Fred admitted. "I'm not a John Lennon who sleeps in bags." The album reached No 6 in the UK.

Another single from Freddie, the ballad 'Made In Heaven', was released at the start of July but reached only 57 despite its lavish video. In the US 'Living On My Own' was the single and that edged up to No 85.

July also saw renewed Queen activity. Christmas 84 had seen a group charity song called 'Do They Know It's Christmas' top the UK singles chart. It was performed by an act called Band Aid, an amalgam of all the current pop stars – George Michael, Duran Duran, Boy George, Phil Collins and Paul Weller et al – designed to raise money for the starving in Ethiopia. The mastermind behind the single, ex-Boomtown Rats front man Bob Geldof, had now set his sights on staging a charity concert at Wembley and Philadelphia to help the third world. It was to be called Live Aid and he wanted rock's leading names to carry the torch – these young pretenders were fine on record, but when it came to putting bums on seats at a concert, the old guard were essential. Queen originally said no to Live Aid; they'd done too many charity gigs that had backfired on them. But once they realised it was being touted as the 'Global Jukebox' and that stars the calibre of David Bowie, Mick Jagger and the Who were taking part they

Main picture: **The miracle**

Picture (above): **"I think anybody who meets Freddie would be in for quite a surprise. He's not quite the prima donna you might imagine. When all is said and done he works damned hard and puts on a good show" – Roger**

found the temptation too great to resist. As Geldof said, "It was the perfect stage for Freddie. The whole world was watching."

The 13 July was a landmark in music. After days of downcast weather the sun shone; after months of planning and promises, the stage was set; and after generations of petulant bickering the world's finest musicians left their egos at home and set out with one mind to do something for others worse off than themselves.

Once committed, Queen approached the show with their customary thoroughness, determined to shine. For three days prior to the event they rehearsed their proposed set, even though they were still fresh from touring Japan (a marked contrast to the Who who allegedly practised for about 15 minutes despite not working together for many years). Each act was allotted just 17 minutes; Queen had to make them count.

While other artists used the global stage just to plug their new product, Queen really got into the idea of the jukebox. "Geldof called Live Aid a jukebox," Brian recalls, "so it seemed obvious to us to simply play the hits and get off." At just after 6 o'clock UK time, Queen took to the stage with no soundcheck and no lights to help them. As soon as Freddie played the opening bars of 'Bohemian Rhapsody' he knew he had the Wembley audience in his hand. By the time the song segued tightly into 'Radio Ga Ga' there was no escaping. Freddie Mercury was a beacon of light, drawing every member of the 72,000 strong crowd towards him with his flamboyant posturings. Any resistance finally melted for good as 144,000 arms clapped perfectly in time to the song. This was his day.

In the wings Jim Hutton watched the man he described touchingly as "my man" hold the world in the palm of his hand. Not a music fan, Jim had little idea of Freddie's status in the business, and he had certainly never seen him perform live. On 13 July he witnessed Freddie at the height of his powers and felt prouder than he'd ever felt in his life. What an introduction!

Jim wasn't the only one impressed; even the band gawped in admiration. Brian: "The rest of us played okay, but Freddie was out there and took it to another level. It wasn't just Queen fans – he connected with everyone." He sure did. After 'Ga Ga', there was the rockingest rendition of 'Crazy Little Thing Called Love', with Fred on his trusty white Tele and Mr Edney on keyboards, plus a blistering 'Hammer To Fall'. Their set ended with an abridged version of 'We Will Rock You' followed by, of course, 'We Are The Champions'. And then they were gone.

Still riding high, Brian and Freddie returned to the stage almost four hours later as Mercury and May to perform one of the most touching moments of the show. With just Brian's acoustic guitar behind him, Freddie managed to sing 'Is This The World We Created?' to the emotional crowd; it was a highly charged moment, soured only by electronic problems which saw the broadcast interrupted by the sound of various directors' voices barking instructions.

The repercussions of the show were manifold. After a hectic period in their careers, Queen now felt revitalised and keen to get back to working together. John: "It was the one day that I was proud to be in the music business. It was a good morale booster for us too, because it showed us the strength of support we had in England and it showed us what we had to offer as a band." Not only that, it showed to millions of viewers around the world what Queen had been offering for 10 years, resulting in massive sales increases in all their records – *Greatest Hits*, for example, leapt an astonishing 72 places.

Despite their re-energised vigour, the next few months were spent on pre-planned solo projects, with the Taylor/Richards partnership producing a German artist called Camy Todorow plus Jason Bonham's band Virginia Wolf, Roger and John guesting on a couple of Elton John tracks, and Freddie releasing another solo single, 'Living On My Own' (the video for which contained scenes from Freddie's 39th birthday party where everyone apart from the host came in drag; unfortunately CBS refused to release the video). Everyone was busy, but nobody's heart seemed really in any of it. What everyone really wanted was for Queen to start working again as soon as possible. Fortunately, they didn't have to wait long.

In keeping with the spirit of unity exemplified by Live Aid, Queen's first single credited to the whole band was released on 4 November in Britain. 'One Vision' was a response to the day's events, but despite being drawn from the thoughts of Martin Luther King, critics saw it as a shameless exploitation of the concert and demanded that all royalties be handed over to the charity. Brian spoke for all the band when he said, "We do a lot of stuff for charities. But 'One Vision' was a way of getting back to what we're doing and if we didn't run ourselves as a business, we wouldn't be around for the next Live Aid. We're not in the full time business of charity at all. We're in the business of making music which is a good enough end in itself."

'One Vision' vaulted straight to No 7 in the UK (No 2 in the fledgling unofficial 'Network Chart'), no doubt helped by its tongue in cheek video by the Torpedo Twins, Hannes Rossacher and Rudi Dolezal, which saw the band recreate their famous Bo Rap head and shoulders pose before becoming a spy on the wall look at Queen recording.

Work on a new album dominated the next few months, with a few minor projects cropping up here and there for the very much in demand singer. In yet another charity performance, Freddie appeared as a model at a show called Fashion Aid, parading down a catwalk with English rose Jane Seymour. He loved it! Next up he agreed to sing a couple of songs on the soundtrack album to a new musical being put together by good friend Dave Clarke (of The Dave Clarke Five), 'In My Defence' and the title track, 'Time' (both to be sung in the show by Cliff Richard). Finally, another single from *Mr Bad Guy*, 'Love Me Like There's No Tomorrow', was released to almost no reaction, despite cheeky press adverts selling him off the back of another act as "Simply Fred; one man and his piano".

With so much post-Live Aid interest in the band's back catalogue, EMI records couldn't resist finding a new way of raking in even more cash. Their answer was *The Complete Works*, a 13 album collection of all the albums except *Greatest Hits*, repackaged in tasteful white sleeves embossed with gold numerals and raised crests. A world map showing Queen's conquests, a very unsatisfactory discography and an itinerary of every date they had played were also included, but without a doubt the thing that guaranteed a purchase from the Queen faithful was the inclusion of a special record compiling all the B-sides that had never made it onto albums, plus 'One Vision' and 'Thank God It's Christmas'.

Complete Vision alone was the reason most people shelled out the £70 asked for the set; if a new Queen album had been around, demand would have been lower.

That new Queen album was still being worked on into the new year. Obviously gripped by the punishing work ethos, even when they weren't required for the album, most of the band couldn't help wandering into other people's studios. Freddie sang on a track called 'Hold On' for his friend Jo Dare, and knocked out some great vocals for Billy Squier's 'Love Is The Hero', also co-writing another song 'Lady With The Tenor Sax.' Roger (and Dave Richards) produced and sang on Magnum's 'Vigilante' album, while John co-wrote a track with Errol Brown called 'This Is Your Time'.

Somehow they all found the time to finish a Queen album as well. Its inspiration had come the year before from Australian video director Russell Mulcahy who was making Highlander, his second feature film and wanted the band to contribute to the soundtrack. "When I did this film there was only one band in my mind to do the music, and that's Queen," he affirmed at the time. "Queen's music was just right for this film – they have a very keen sense of visuals. They write very powerful, anthem-type songs and the film needed just that kind of energy." Once in the studio they were so inspired that at one time a proper soundtrack to the film was an

Main picture (right):
A kind of magic

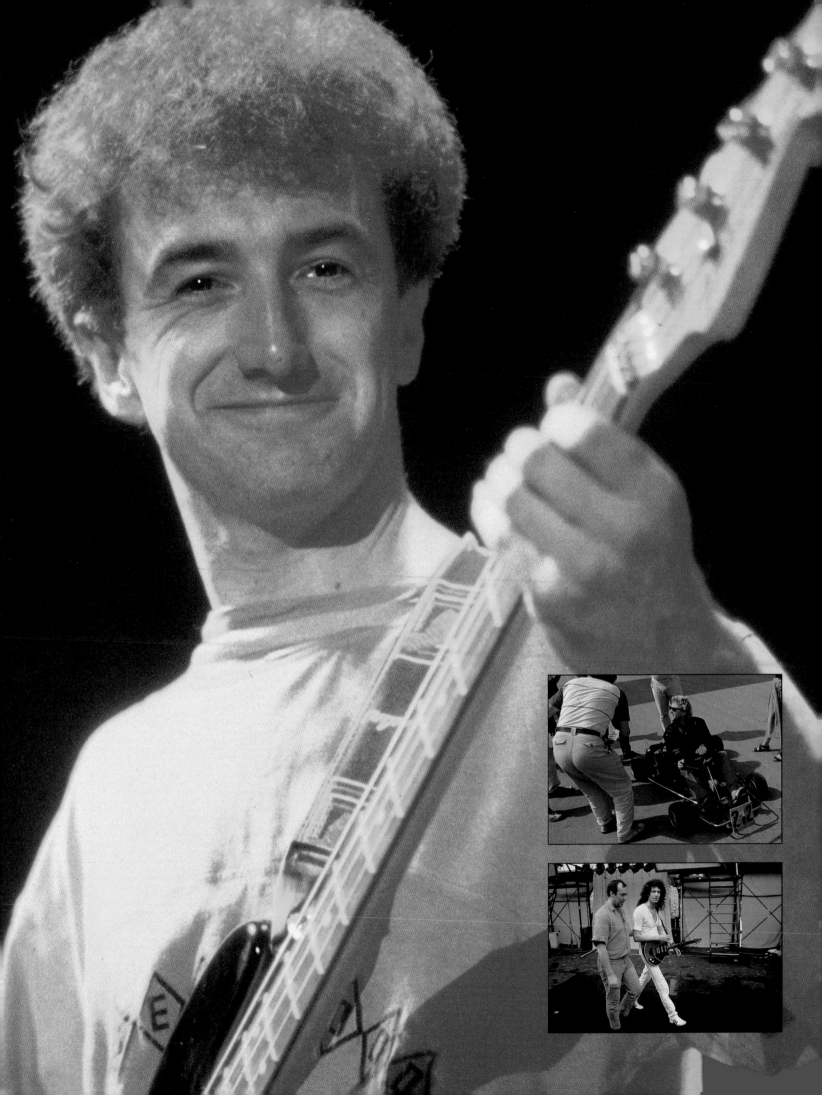

option, but in the end they settled for including the six songs they'd written for it on a fully fledged, 'proper' album. (Highlander eventually featured several film-only mixes of the songs, plus a wondrously haunting snatch of 'New York New York' from an animated Freddie.)

The first fruits of the album were heard in March or April, depending on whether you lived in the UK or US. For Britain, EMI decided to release the album's title track, Roger's 'A Kind Of Magic' (two singles from Roger in as many albums), while Capitol released Fred's complex powerhouse 'Princes Of The Universe' in the States in an attempt to woo back Queen's original rock fans. Each had a lavish video (courtesy of Mr Mulcahy), with Highlander star Christopher Lambert popping up in POTU's to do battle with Fred (a sword against a microphone stand is hardly fair!). The songs took the band back into the Top 3 in Britain – and absolutely nowhere in America.

A Kind Of Magic – the album – wasn't to appear for another month. In the interim John released his first – and last! – solo single under the name The Immortals. The song was called 'No Turning Back' and came from the film Biggles. It never charted so most people were spared the sight of John dressed as Biggles in the video, which also starred Vincent Price. Freddie managed to cause havoc during a showing of Time when he decided to try his hand at selling interval ice creams. When his assistant Joe Fanelli pointed out that "he wouldn't have a clue what a pound coin looked like, so how on earth was he going to give people the right change", Fred's response was typically pragmatic: he bought the whole stock and proceeded to fling ices to all within his sights. Brian, meanwhile, attended the film premiere of *Down And Out In Beverly Hills* where he met Britain's soap actress of the moment, Anita Dobson.

Before the album's release the video for another single, co-written by Freddie and John, was put under wraps. When it emerged in June, 'Friends Will Be Friends' was welcomed by many as an anthemic classic in the vein of 'We Are The Champions', but basic structure aside (both songs run verse/chorus/verse/chorus to fade) it lacks all the majesty of the 1977 hit and appears to be Fred writing by numbers. It is also probably the only hit song to contain the word "lumber".

More than a month before the album's release, real Queen fans got a sneak preview at the band's first official Fan Club convention at Great Yarmouth. (The convention also saw the British premiere of Highlander at a seaside cinema.) The rest of the nation was put out of its misery on 2 June with the release of *A Kind Of Magic*, amazingly Queen's 14th album. Two of the

songs had already been aired as singles, but there were still a couple of surprises left on the nine track album. Only six of the songs were for Highlander in the end ('One Vision' is to be found on the soundtrack to Iron Eagle instead) and they are easily spotted by their respective lyric's tangential suggestions: 'Don't Lose Your Head', 'Who Wants To Live Forever' and 'Gimme The Prize' are direct quotes from the dialogue, for instance.

The album became Queen's first No 1 in Britain (46 in the States) for five years, a fact which pleased EMI. It also pleased the independent label Rough Trade, home of indie darlings The Smiths. The marketing masterminds there had forecast Queen's assault on the summit and planned the release of their group's next album around the fact; wouldn't it be amusing if Queen were actually toppled by an album called *The Queen Is Dead*? In theory yes; in practice, Genesis's *Invisible Touch* stomped in and ruined everybody's plans.

Queen had managed to dodge the depressing album/tour/album/tour cycle for too long, and June saw them commence what was to be their final tour – a fact unappreciated at the time. Stockholm had the honour of opening the 26 date series, marred only by anti-apartheid demonstrators – still! – and appalling weather. As most of the tour's venues were outdoors, clement conditions played a major factor in determining an individual show's success. Performance-wise, the gigs were *Magic* by name, and magic in content with the band pulling off a healthy blend of classics and newies. They had barely left Scandinavia before reports filtered through to the UK press; the show was fine, they all agreed, but what was really newsworthy was Freddie's daring outfit worn to close the set. Based on Napoleon's imperial robes, designer Diane Moseley's ermine lined cloak and bejewelled crown gave the larger than life singer the perfect image to show the world. He was the King of Rock Music and no mistake.

Like other monarchs before him, Freddie swept through Europe

Main picture: **Despite his hectic holiday schedule John has found time to work with John McEnroe, Errol Brown, Vincent Price and Morris Minor And The Majors among others**

Insert picture (top): **While Freddie toured art galleries and museums and Brian went hot air ballooning, Roger did a few laps of Budapest's go kart track**

Insert picture (bottom): **On a flight to America Brian paid for the Red Special to have its own seat next to him because he didn't trust the aircraft's hold**

claiming territory after territory as his own. By the time his campaign roadshow reached home, tales of his conquests had whipped the whole country into a state of feverish expectation. eventually reaching home. They began with what was almost an intimate warm up gig by their standards – a mere 38,000 audience at St James's Park in Newcastle. The event had broken the stadium's box office records by selling out in hours, a fact the Save The Children Fund were grateful for since all the show's profits were donated to the charity.

London was where Queen were happiest, however. After the previous year's triumph, two nights at Wembley almost felt like coming home. Freddie was on top form – he had to be because the Saturday show was being filmed – and the weather just about behaved itself after soaking a couple of the support acts (one of whom was INXS, recent headliners there in their own right). One of the highlights for the fans came during 'A Kind Of Magic' when four giant dirigibles based on the caricatures on the cover of the album were suddenly inflated. Within minutes on the Saturday two of the balloons were mauled to destruction by the crowd, while Fred's inflatable effigy broke loose of its mooring ropes to land miles away (it currently resides in a box at the home of one of the authors!). The show didn't stop with the final encore that night, as the band moved on to their own party at Kensington's Roof Gardens. Under the guise of Dicky Heart And The Pacemakers they blasted through a short rock'n'roll set for the amassed party goers, joined on stage by the likes of Gary Glitter and ex-topless model Samantha Fox.

Manchester followed, then Cologne, Vienna and Budapest. Hungary, like all Iron Curtain states, had been off limits to such decadence as rock acts under the strict laws of Stalinist Moscow, but with Gorbachev in power much more was possible. So it was that Queen played to a Nepstadion packed with fans from all over the Eastern Bloc. To commemorate the triumph, Freddie and Brian played an emotion charged Hungarian folk song called Tavaski Szel to the bowled over throng – eagle eyed viewers of the video of the show will see Fred reading the words from his hand; but it's the thought that counts! By the time they left Budapest, another special relationship with a previously ignored country had been formed. "We had a wonderful time in Hungary," Roger remembers. "I think everyone who came to the Nepstadion enjoyed themselves. Especially our support! It was about 60 middle aged ladies in the traditional costume, singing a Hungarian folklore version of Jumpin' Jack Flash and, believe me, it was different!"

France and Spain were next to succumb to the galloping rockfest, and then there was just one more show. On 9 August Knebworth Park and all its surrounding roads ground to a halt as their majesties' bandwagon dominated the entire area. Quite sensibly the band chose to fly in, which they did in a gaudily customised *A Kind Of Magic* helicopter right in the middle of support act Big Country's set; as soon as the crowd saw the chopper overhead their excited cheers signalled once and for all to Mr Adamson and friends that the 120,000 strong audience were there for one reason; and that reason was just about to land.

The tour was an unmitigated success: total audiences topped more than a million (400,000 in the UK alone), the tour grossed £11,000,000 and set attendance records in every country they played. The stage was the largest construction many venues had ever seen and half a continent could confirm Taylor's pre-tour boast that the shows would be "bigger than bigness itself. It'll make Ben Hur look like The Muppets." But there were a couple of dampeners on the jubilation. At Knebworth a Status Quo fan was fatally stabbed; and, while everyone's lives were inextricably altered by the tour, John in particular ended it a less happily married man than he started it.

With the tour finished and personal problems to the fore, 1987 was declared another rest year. That still left half of 1986 to be used as each member saw fit. Freddie finally decided it was time he made use of the beautiful Kensington home he'd bought six years earlier and moved in with his small entourage, Jim Hutton and an army of cats. (The album credit on *Mr Bad Guy* had read: "This album is dedicated to cat lovers everywhere. Screw everybody else!") Brian meanwhile divided his time between denying rumours surrounding his relationship with Anita Dobson, producing Japanese artist Minako Honda on her *Cancelled* album (John also appeared) and playing with rock'n'roll satirists Bad News.

Main picture: *"On stage I'm a big macho, sexual object and I'm very arrogant, so most people dismiss me because of that. They don't know what I'm really like"* – Freddie

Background picture: *For his two hours on stage, Freddie was a man possessed, a 5'9" figure who became a giant in front of an audience. He used that short time to enrich the lives of everyone around him*

Without much help from them, the Queen machine trundled ever forwards. 15 September saw Brian's 'Who Wants To Live Forever' released in the UK (it reached No 24), while American audiences were given the chance to ignore another Mercury/Deacon collaboration 'Pain Is So Close To Pleasure' (which they did; it failed to chart). The video to WWTLF plus that of 'A Kind Of Magic 'made history when it was released as a video single – another first for the band. The next month saw further barriers being broken as Queen secured the first ever simultaneous hook up of an independent television station – Channel 4 – with all local radios nationally for the first public airing of the 12 July concert under the banner Real Magic. Approximately 3.5 million people tuned in that night, clocking up Queen's largest ever audience in Britain.

Fans were given a further chance to relive the Magic Tour with the release of the band's second live album, *Live Magic* on 1 December. Many critics surprisingly were impressed, but it didn't fool Queen fans. The problem? Well, in order to restrict the album to a single disc while still retaining as much of the show as possible, someone somewhere took the decision to cut the songs. Not only is the opera section of 'Bo Rap' discarded like an old manager, but 'We Are The Champions', 'We Will Rock You' and 'Tie Your Mother Down' all suffer the dreaded edit; 'Tie Your Mother Down' suffers more than most due to its alternate chorus – where Fred sings "All your love tonight" and expects the repeated response, what he actually gets is a line from the next chorus, "Ain't no friend of mine." Terrible. But to the 400,000 people who saw the concerts in the UK it proved an irresistible memento; spookily, 400,000 copies were sold – and all without a single. Queen had done it again.

All may have been quiet on the Queen front, but the solace stopped there. Brian's activity was personal; he was suffering the full glare of the British tabloids intent on knowing every detail of his increasingly public affair with Anita Dobson. His second daughter Emily Ruth was born in the middle of it all.

Freddie's activity was purely work related in early 1987. Inspired by the previous year's successes he had returned eagerly to the studio (this time Townhouse in London) to work on further solo material. The first result of his labours was a marvellously camp rendition of the old Platters number, 'The Great Pretender', with Freddie backing himself in a multitrack heaven. For the song's video he decided he couldn't mime to all the parts and so drafted in Roger and old chum Peter Straker. It was then he revealed he wanted female backing singers! The sight of Messrs Mercury, Taylor and Straker pretending to be Mss Mercury, Taylor and Straker proved one of the video highlights of a career full of them. The single reached No 4 in the UK; it also marked the end of Freddie's moustachioed image.

While Freddie may have been inspired by the band's 'magic year', one influential organisation wasn't. When the British Phonographic Industry announced its nominees for the UK equivalent of the Grammys, Queen were passed over for acts who had done less, sold fewer and who had already begun the slide into obscurity. In order to ram the point home, EMI took out an ad in the ceremony's programme designed to point out just a fraction of the band's achievements in 1986:

1 Queen sold 1,774,991 albums in the UK alone.
2 *A Kind Of Magic* entered the UK album chart at No 1 and remained in the Top 5 for 13 consecutive weeks.
3 The 1,828,375th fan in the UK bought a copy of Queen's *Greatest Hits*, and the album continued in the UK Top 100 charts throughout the year, where it has been for 268 weeks.
4 Queen sold out two nights at Wembley Stadium, one night at Newcastle St James's Park, one night at Manchester Maine Road and one night at Knebworth – total in excess of 400,000 people – an all time UK attendance record.
5 Queen's Real Magic, directed by Gavin Taylor, became the first ever stereo simulcast on independent television and the independent radio network when a satellite link up took place on 25 October.
6 Queen's 657th performance became the first ever major stadium concert in the Eastern Bloc on 27 July at the Nepstadion in Budapest, filmed with 17 35mm movie cameras by the Hungarian State Film Agency, Mafilm.
7 *Queen's Magic In Budapest*, directed by Janos Zsombolyai, became the first full length feature concert film to be premiered in the Eastern Bloc in Budapest's National Congress Hall on 12 December.
8 Queen released their first ever video single in the UK, entering the video charts at No 1 on 27 October.
9 Queen's Magic Tour of Europe played to over 1 million people in June, July and August in 26 dates, grossing in excess of £11,000,000.
10 *Daily Mirror* readers voted Queen the Best Band of 1986 by 50% votes more than any other band.
11 *Daily Mirror* readers voted Freddie Mercury Best Male Vocalist for 1986 "by miles".
12 Freddie Mercury's video EP entered the UK video chart at No 1 on 21 July.
13 Queen held their first ever three day Fan Club convention at Great Yarmouth on 25 April.
14 Russell Mulcahy's second feature film, *Highlander*, with a music score by Queen and Michael Kamen went on general release in the UK on 29 August.
15 Queen threw 28 parties.
16 Queen gave the proceeds of their Newcastle Football Ground concert to the Save The Children Fund.
17 Richard Gray spent 918 hours working on Queen artwork and

Main picture: **"You buggers can sing higher than I can, I tell ya!"**

Insert: **"We've all been hauled through the tabloids now. It's not been pleasant. Some papers want a certain kind of news and it can wreck people's lives and I don't think they have any sense of responsibility about it"**

received Best Album Cover award from *The Daily Express*.

18 Queen released *Live Magic* on 1 December and sold over 400,000 before Christmas without a single.

19 Queen hits were released on no fewer than 53 compilation albums in 23 countries throughout the world.

20 Freddie Mercury was 40.

21 Queen refused to ban their videos from appearing on British television.

22 Queen Films had five videos in the UK Top 25 on 8 November.

23 Freddie Mercury was voted Best Male Vocalist of the year by readers of *The Sun*.

24 Queen were voted Best Group of the year by Capital Radio listeners.

25 Mary Turner described Queen as a national institution.

26 Queen's 'We Will Rock You' entered the *Music Week* Top 10 video charts in July where it remained for the rest of the year.

27 Queen's Greatest Flix remained in the *Music Week* Top 30 video charts all year totalling 115 consecutive weeks since being

Background picture: The official attendance at Knebworth was 120,000, but police estimates suggested double that

Insert picture (this page): Mr Bad Guy

Insert picture (opposite page): Brian, Freddie, Roger and Spike aboard President Gorbachev's personal hydrofoil

the first ever No 1 video in the UK.

28 Queen's Live In Rio remained in the Music Week Top 30 video charts all year, totalling 80 consecutive weeks since its debut at No 1 on 20 May 1985.

29 Queen were awarded Top Music Video for Live In Rio at the British Video Awards on 16 October.

30 Shell adopted 'I Want To Break Free' as their main theme song for a nationwide television and radio campaign.

31 Hannes Rossacher and Rudi Dolezal nearly finished post-production on their mammoth video cassette Queen – Magic Years (A Visual Anthology) – due for release early 1987.

32 Yet again Queen fail to win a BPI Award.

Thank you Brian, John, Freddie and Roger – we at EMI appreciate you.

While their record company defended the group's honour, its individual parts had solo matters to attend to. At the end of May Freddie unveiled his grandest and most adventurous project yet: an operatic single with the legendary Catalan diva Montserrat Caballé. He had been a fan of hers for years and when the chance came to meet her in Spain during the tour he had leapt at it. "I just thought, and still think, that she has a marvellous voice," he said later, "and on Spanish television I happened to mention it and she came to hear it, called me up and said, Let's do something together. So we met in Barcelona and the story unfolds from there."

With Mike Moran Freddie had written two tracks, one called 'Exercises In Free Love' (which had appeared as the B-side to The 'Great Pretender') and another called 'Barcelona'. Monty, as Freddie soon called her, loved both songs and together they committed themselves to recording a whole album. Freddie and Mike would write and arrange the songs and Montserrat would arrive and lay down her vocals usually in one take. At Ibiza's Ku Club the unlikely duo previewed Barcelona to a stunned crowd that had just sat through Duran Duran and Spandau Ballet and closed the show to rapturous applause and a sensational firework display.

Brian in the meantime was working with a different style of singer. As well as tackling production chores for Ms Dobson, he was writing several songs for her album. 'Talking Of Love', the first single, helped their attempt at hiding their affair not one jot. When the pair appeared together on UK chat show Wogan, they were still denying what was obvious to most, for the sake of Brian's family. He had also dipped another toe into production waters by agreeing to sit behind the desk for Bad News, even helping to record a version of 'Bohemian Rhapsody' (which actually reached No 44), as well as finding time to record a charity song, 'A Time For Heroes', with Meat Loaf.

Roger too had ambitions outside of Queen. Two solo albums down the line he felt ready to do another one, but with a twist. He wanted to do his next project as part of a proper band and so auditioned 250 musicians anonymously, before selecting Peter Noone (bass), Joshua Macrae (drums – yes, really!) and Clayton Moss (guitar). Roger would handle rhythm guitar duties plus occasional sticks sessions, with fifth Queen member Spike Edney bringing up the rear with his multi-instrumental skills.

The Cross, as they eventually became known after the usual arguments, commenced rehearsals immediately before being whisked off to Ibiza, scene of Fred's recent success, to add their own contributions to the solo album Roger had virtually completed. More than ever, Roger was a dedicated member of Queen, but after the previous year's frenetic activity he needed to busy himself again. "Queen is like a huge rolling machine," he confessed at the time, "and we're not working all the time. I am a musician by profession – that's my whole life. I don't want to waste it." Later he added: "I want to play music I sincerely believe in, and I want to do it live. The solo LPs were my own expression of my own musical product at the time. This is a whole new group which is going to be taken seriously, I hope. This is a whole new career."

The success of 'Barcelona' in its Iberian homeland was unparalleled. Record shops' stocks were completely depleted and the Spanish Government immediately appropriated the song to be used as the official theme to 1992's Olympic Games (in the end, perhaps to avoid connection with something as controversial as AIDS, they replaced the song with a new Andrew Lloyd Webber composition...). Britain's reaction was no less impressive: "This is sensational. Quite extraordinary and the ultimate in high camp" was the verdict of heavy metal bible Kerrang. "This will appeal to real music lovers" opined Sounds. Freddie was less sure. "I don't know how Queen fans will react to this," he admitted. "I'll have to find out. It is a bit of a thingy... you can't put it under a label can you? The worst thing they can call it is 'rock opera', which is so boring actually." The song shot to No 8 in the UK.

On a darker side, at least in hindsight, Freddie chose late 87 to speak publicly for the first time about his sex life. "I lived for sex," he confessed. "Amazingly I've just gone completely the other way. AIDS changed my life – I have stopped going out, I've become almost a nun. I was extremely promiscuous but I've stopped all that. What's more I don't miss that kind of life. Anyone who has been promiscuous should have a test. I'm fine,

I'm clear." A couple of years earlier his raison d'être had been extremely different: "I'm just an old slag who gets up every morning, scratches his head and wonders who he wants to fuck." His calming down can be attributed in a large part to the love of a good man (although in his brilliant, and shockingly moving memoirs Jim Hutton reveals that Freddie occasionally fell off the sexual wagon every now and again).

The relationship between Freddie and Mary Austin had been over physically for a decade, but they were still the closest of friends and she continued working closely with him from within the Queen organisation. Proof of their enduring closeness came in January when they were both called upon to be witnesses at the wedding of Roger and Dominique. The 25 January wedding was not all it seemed, however, and 23 days later Roger moved out of the family home to be with girlfriend Debbie Leng. The Taylors' relationship had been over for a while, but Roger wanted to ensure his children's financial security, hence the nuptials.

Rock'n'roll had claimed another marriage. Roger and 'Flake girl Debbie' (as the tabloids referred to her since she was featured at the time in a television campaign for the chocolate bar), had met during a video shoot for The Cross's first single, 'Cowboys And Indians' the year before. Now as the album was released they were still together.

In most instances, a decent bout of controversy gives new releases a healthy shot in the arm. But despite Roger's face being splashed all over newspaper front pages for days, the album Shove It did very poorly. It struggled to No 58 in the UK (athletic by its US counterpart's standards) and the singles fared no better. Despite the presence of a band, the album is purely Roger, and arguably not very good Roger at that. The gains of Strange Frontier seemed to be lost, although there were some wonderful moments. 'Heaven For Everyone' featured a classic pull-out-all-the-stops guest vocal

from Fred, while 'Love Lies Bleeding' had a solo from Brian. But lively exuberances like 'Stand Up For Love' were few and far between on an album dominated by rhythm heavy plodders like the title track, 'Rough Justice' and 'Contact' (the American record featured the wonderful 'Feel The Force'). Still, the music press liked it: "A nifty little début and, I'm sure, the start of a fruitful new era in Roger Taylor's career" was the verdict of a particularly enamoured (female) *NME* reviewer, while Kerrang less passionately pointed out that "judged objectively and on its own terms, this debut is a beautifully produced slab of super sophisticated pop rock".

Phase two of Taylor's supra-Queen designs swung into action with a low key tour of Britain. Audiences were small but impressed. Roger was actually seen to have legs after all those years stuck behind a drum kit and what's more he played some mean rhythm guitar around Clayton's increasingly Hendrix inspired licks. The inclusion of 'Let's Get Crazy' from *Fun In Space* and a storming 'Man On Fire' from *Strange Frontier* were unexpected treats, but the finale of 'I'm In Love With My Car' really struck home. Of the new material, 'Stand Up For Love' screamed single – and was ignored. The band hardly set attendance records anywhere but they did have one power coup at the Montreux Festival. They refused to mime and held out until permission was granted to play live – Roger still had some clout in the town, although the fact that Jim Beach was behind the event didn't hurt.

The rest of Queen popped up a couple of times for their own live shows soon after – but only for charity. Freddie turned in a dazzling display during a special performance of 'Time' at London's Dominion Theatre while John and Brian formed part of the house band at 1988's Prince's Trust concert, performing alongside Eric Clapton, Phil Collins and Joe Cocker – a personal favourite of Brian's.

Freddie almost made another live appearance at the magical La Nit festival to promote Barcelona's Olympic festivities on 8 October in front of the King and Queen of Spain – he was there in body but demanded that he and Montserrat mime. "We'd need a lot of rehearsals," he defended. "They're complex songs and we just didn't have enough time." The songs in question were Barcelona plus two new tracks from the forthcoming album, 'How Can I Go On' and 'The Golden Boy'. Two days later the duo swept into London's Royal Opera House for the album's official launch; Radio One disc jockey Simon Bates mentioned it briefly on his morning show and so a small army of dedicated Fredophiles descended on Covent Garden hoping to catch a glimpse of their idol. They weren't disappointed, as Freddie and Montserrat

arrived in regal style in a chauffeur driven blue Rolls-Royce to meet the assembled throng of media pundits grateful for the free flowing champagne (it didn't stop most of them slating the album though).

A month later the final results of Brian's own duet with a female star came to light with the release of Anita Dobson's *Talking Of Love* album. Brian attempted to head off criticism early on. "I think we produced an album that strides across the two worlds in which we live," he explained. "There's a certain amount of rock influence and a certain amount of show influence. I stand by the project as being very worthwhile." The press furore over their private lives continued unabated. Eventually enough was enough and Brian made the decision he hoped he would never have to make; after much soul searching he moved out of his marital home, away from his wife and, more importantly, his children to start afresh with Anita. It should have been a relief, but press interest removed almost all of the pleasure; his father's death on 2 June exacerbated his turmoil and he sank into depression. Things had to get better.

As well as her solo album, the recovered Brian also contributed to the soundtrack of Anita's next project, the stage play Budgie. He also found time to play on tracks by Holly Johnson, 'Living In A Box', Steve Hackett, 'Fuzzbox', Black Sabbath and Lonnie Donegan (for whom he wrote 'Let Your Heart Rule Your Head', later to pop up on his own solo album). He also jammed with Elton John at a Bon Jovi gig (where he didn't use the Red Special) and appeared alongside The Cross and the reclusive John Deacon at a Queen Fan Club Christmas party at Hammersmith Palais. Three members of Queen in public together was something that hadn't been seen since Knebworth two years earlier, and it inspired the same question in everyone: are you ready, Freddie?

Main picture: **A recording of Queen's 12 July 1986 show got to No 2 in May 1992**

Picture (above): **"The bigger the better – in everything"**

HANG ON IN THERE

Freddie was actually ready, and had been for some time. He didn't want to see another Queen tour just yet, but he had been back in the studio, on and off, with the whole band since the previous January. Now, January 1989, their 16th album was complete and ready for a spring release (they had missed out on the hoped for Christmas deadline).

The release of 'I Want It All' on 2 May saw Queen's first single for three years and their 32nd (in the UK) in total. The song kicked off with a rousing a cappella chorus before the rest of the band flew in, guitars diving and weaving, drums pounding and pushing in a gorgeous swirling aural mass. Freddie's voice reached out with all the passion and fury usually saved for touring, adding to the distinctly heavy overall tone. On first listen you knew it was a Brian song in the vein of 'Hammer To Fall', but a look at the disc's credit revealed something quite different.

'Queen' was the name of the official writers; at last, after years of squabbling about credits, royalties and song selection, the band had taken a step they should have taken years earlier and credited a

Main picture (right): **"In the larger venues you tend to lose that intimacy, but on the other hand you gain something else. You get the feeling of an event and the more people there are, the greater the tension becomes"**

Picture (above): **Freddie limbering up backstage at Slane Castle, 1986**

song to the four of them. The B-side, 'Hang On In There', was the same: 'Queen', read the writer's credit. It was a theme that extended all the way through the new album, called *The Miracle*, when it came on 22 May, and there was a very good reason for it. "We wanted to record a really democratic album, where each one of us would be involved in the songwriting," explained Brian on its release. "The consequence was that no one was only partially involved, because each track is credited to all four musicians. Regardless of who had the basic idea for the song, we were all involved and worked on it to the same extent, so we created a real band feeling without any ego problems. That's one of the reasons that *The Miracle* has turned into such a better album than *A Kind Of Magic*." In the main, it was a successful exercise with just the odd scuffle. "It was okay, but we had our various fisticuffs," revealed Freddie.

The new songwriting parity may have helped group spirits, but it also provided a new game for fans: working out who really wrote what. While Brian is obviously the originator of the first single, Roger is the main force behind 'The Invisible Man' (only he would be that trendy) and 'Breakthru' (although Fred contributed the operatic intro). 'My Baby Does Me' can be traced back to 'Cool Cat' – obviously the Deacon/Mercury alliance in full effect – while 'The Miracle' is as close to pure Mercury as you can get. And so it goes on, with each song offering little clues. The album's opening cuts, 'Party' and 'Khashoggi's Ship', are obviously more the result of band jamming sessions than a premeditated writing session. (Note to Queen fans: one way of tracing a song's origins is to listen out for the backing vocals. Although it is often a three person harmony, one voice is usually dominant, like Freddie's on the intro to 'Breakthru' or Roger's throughout 'The Invisible Man'. Going back further, 'Radio Ga Ga' (Taylor's song) clearly has the drummer's vocals accentuated on the choruses; 'Tie Your Mother Down' pushes Brian in the same way. It's not an infallible method, but it does have some merit!)

The newfound unity in the studio extended to the album's artwork. Richard Gray, the mastermind behind the distinctive *A Kind Of Magic* cover, was approached early on in the year to repeat his success with the band. In a meeting with the group he was instructed to conjure up a design that amalgamated a portrait shot of each member into one head, "to give a visual image of the organic working unit we felt we had become" according to Brian. Gray achieved his target with the help of a Quantel Graphic Paintbox and hours of work. The result? Sensational; a cover with four heads seeping seamlessly into each other. The eerie design was so popular it was used as the basis to the artwork adorning each single release.

Speaking of singles, the next promotional tool for the album (which had immediately hit No 1 in the UK and a record 26 in the States) was 'Breakthru'. The song's pumping, breathy rhythm suggested many ideas for a video, but finally a printable one was adopted and so the band trotted off to the Nene Valley Railway in Cambridgeshire to be filmed performing on the back of a moving train. Freddie looks superb throughout the film, a smack in the face for the rumour mongers who were beginning to suggest he was becoming frail through illness (his old friend Nicolai Grishanovitch had died from AIDS earlier in the year).

While the band were fully back as a recording unit, their history as a live act looked unlikely to be added to, with Freddie abjectly refusing to go out on the road. "I want to change the cycle of album, world tour, album, world tour," he insisted during a Radio One interview with DJ Mike Read. "Maybe we will tour, but it will be for totally different reasons. I've personally had it with these bombastic lights and staging effects. I don't think a 42 year old man should be running around in his leotard anymore." The rest of the band were as diplomatic as possible about the decision, but it hurt them not to be playing after such a long break. As far as the media scavengers were concerned, it was further 'proof' that something was amiss with Freddie (but then the same people said that the whole album cover design had been a stunt to hide the singer's gaunt looks; his new beard was a similar device, they claimed). The innuendoes were refuted by Roger: "Stupid rumours! Freddie is as healthy as ever on the new album. We had a party at Brian's a few days ago and Freddie didn't exactly give the impression he was on his death bed."

In the absence of a tour, another single, 'The Invisible Man', consolidated Queen's success. A synth heavy workout, it is remarkable for featuring all four members' names being called out before an appropriate solo. It was also the hippest thing from Queen in a long while, although by no means a direct attempt at being trendy. "It would be bloody ridiculous if Queen made a record using acid house techniques," Roger exclaimed. "It would be jumping on bandwagons, and we've never been ones for that."

In remarkable contrast to *The Works* policy of draining the album dry, and *A Kind Of Magic* approach of re-airing classic tracks, from 'I Want It All' onwards, Queen's singles featured new songs as B-sides – even CD versions of the album had an extra track, the aptly named 'Chinese Torture'. After 'Hang On In There' came 'Stealin'' – a scat attack, Queen style – on Breakthru's other side, while 'The Invisible Man' was supported by the Roger sung (no guesses for who wrote it!) 'Hijack My Heart'. The band's next single, 'Scandal', was underwritten by the quirky 'My Life Has Been Saved', but unfortunately by the time of the record fifth single from the album, the pot was empty and fans had to be content with an unreleased live cut of 'Stone Cold Crazy' – some second prize!

More previously unavailable material came on a new video called Rare Live – A Concert Through Time And Space. Compiled by the Torpedo Twins, it assembled footage from gigs throughout the band's career. Much of it is excellent – certainly the band are hot in every clip – but there seems too much fancy editing for its own sake. Perhaps in an attempt to cram as much in as possible, the video switches constantly from one performance to another mid song, a technique which worked in moderation on the 'We Will Rock You' opening sequence on the same team's remarkable Magic Years collection. Also, the inclusion of widely available clips from the 1986 Wembley and Budapest shows seems unnecessary, as does the appearance of so much Live Aid film – nobody could have missed that!

Something else which could not go unnoticed was Roger's 40th birthday. To celebrate in style he erected two large marquees in the garden of his rather magnificent Surrey home (Ian Hunter later said that if you added Roger's place to Phil Collins', there wouldn't be much of Surrey left) and arranged a coach relay to ship guests to and from London. As well as the monstrous lighting rig for two live bands, he decided to put the celebration on the map by hiring a Sky Tracker industrial spotlight, for which he also needed a licence from the Civil Aviation Authority who needed to warn planes not to think there was a landing strip below! Unfortunately he didn't inform the locals, so for most of the night several police forces were called to investigate the many sightings of massive light emissions, believed to emanate from an invading alien fleet! Once again, Roger made the front pages in the UK press.

The remainder of 1989 was split between working on new material for individual projects and looking back over Queen's golden past. Roger flew out to Switzerland to work on The Cross's second album, John and family disappeared to their apartment in Biarritz (seemingly rarely to emerge), while Brian gigged with anyone who looked at him. With Roger he worked on a charity single for Armenia – a version of 'Smoke On The Water' – with David Gilmour, Tony Iommi, Paul Rodgers and Bruce Dickinson among others; he also played with Artists United For Nature, Buddy star Gareth Marks, Jerry Lee Lewis and two children called Ian and Belinda who had recorded a special version of 'Who Wants To Live Forever' for his bone marrow charity. Brian even found time to break his arm in a skateboarding accident – and at his age!

In December the Band Of Joy label released those old sessions Queen had done for the BBC way back when, under the illuminating title of *Queen At The Beeb*. The album comprised the band's two four track appearances and gave new fans a rare insight into the ambitious, unpolished ensemble Queen had once been.

Further cause for retrospection came with the results of various end of decade polls. Above all the rest, Queen were most delighted to scoop Best Group Of The 80s during ITV's Goodbye To The 80s show, hosted by Cilla Black, because it had been voted for by viewers of the station and readers of *TV Times* magazine – in other words, real people, not some elusive panel of so-called experts. The whole band – even Freddie – turned up to collect the prestigious award. They had seen out their second decade in the same position as they had their first – at the top.

Main picture: "When you're on stage there's such a communication thing going on with the audience that when you come off there's a terrible void, an empty feeling, and all you want to do is get close to lots of people again"

Picture (above): "Freddie always looked like a star and acted like a star even though he was penniless" – Brian

1990, 18 February, the same British Phonographic Industry that had ignored Queen in 1987 presented the band with a special award for Outstanding Contribution To Music. Once again the entire group turned out to pick up the honour. Brian and Roger handled the acceptance speech side of things while John and the increasingly thin looking Freddie smiled in the background (Fred did say "thankyou" into the microphone as he walked off stage). A short video tribute was played to commemorate their career.

After the ceremony the guests of honour avoided the special BPI dinner in favour of a visit to Groucho's nightclub in Soho. They had booked the entire club for a private party to celebrate the small matter of their 20th year as Queen (although John had only been on the scene a mere 19 years). 400 specially invited guests, from old roadies to managers to secretaries piled into the venue

for a magnificent night to remember. The band were presented with a giant cake in the shape of a monopoly board, and photographed for all the world to see. Unfortunately most tabloids chose to run pictures of Freddie leaving the bash in the early hours not looking his best and put their own comment into the reason for his stricken looks. Soon afterwards

Main picture: **The Mercury/Deacon songwriting partnership was responsible for some of Queen's most stylish tracks**

Picture (above): **'I Want To Break Free', 'Another One Bites The Dust', 'Spread Your Wings' and 'You're My Best Friend' were all written by John**

he issued a statement denying he was ill; but the murmuring continued.

Queen had obviously come a long way in 20 years because, for the party, Roger bought Debbie Leng an antique necklace worth £150,000. Were he to have relied on his earnings from 'The Cross' she may had to have settled for something slightly less extravagant – their new album, *Mad, Bad And Dangerous To Know* was released in March to hardly any sales in the UK and only a few more in Germany. A pity, since it was far superior to the band's début effort, with each member having a go at the dreaded business of songwriting. This time round Roger's tracks were restricted to two, but they were each corkers. 'Old Men' began his lengthy ascent into political comment with subtlety and aplomb, while 'Final Destination' closed the album with suitable class. A cover of Hendrix's 'Foxy Lady' allowed Clayton to really show what he was capable of – and who inspired him to do it – while the opening riff to 'On Top Of The World Ma' perhaps paid homage rather too well to Led Zeppelin's 'Whole Lotta Love'. But easily the star of the show was the chant-a-long 'Power To Love', the first single from the selection. Sadly, it failed to chart in the UK, and the band were only allowed to tour Germany to support it. A second single, 'Liar', suffered a similar fate, as did the third, 'Final Destination', despite having a live version of 'Man On Fire' on its B-side. Another blow came to Roger's year with his father's death in July. They hadn't been close, but perhaps that made coming to terms with it harder.

Another tribute to how good the last couple of decades had been to Queen was in evidence when Jim Beach bought the band's entire back catalogue from Capitol for an undisclosed but obviously considerable sum. The search for a new American company was on. The winning bidders came in the unlikely shape of the Disney organisation who were setting up a record label, Hollywood Records. They felt that owning Queen's phenomenal back catalogue would be a fitting start, and duly handed over £10,000,000 for the privilege.

Queen had been back in the studio at various times since Christmas 89, but work was not consistent and Brian, as usual, found time to squeeze in the odd outside project or six. At the start of the year he'd helped out on yet another charity effort, a version of Rod Stewart's 'Sailing' for the Rock Against Repatriation project, swiftly followed by an appearance alongside Ian Hunter and Mick Ronson at the Hammersmith Odeon, an onstage jam with Black Sabbath (same venue), some guitar work for new band D-Rock and initial work on the soundtrack to a production of Macbeth (to be put on in Hammersmith, of course). He also popped up alongside The Cross for another Fan Club Christmas extravaganza, where, for the first time, he and Roger

Commencing with an audible count in, Roger begins a bolero rhythm that pervades most of the song, before making way for Steve Howe's "wandering minstrel" acoustic showcase and Brian's heavy metal denouement. The song is once again attributed to the group as a whole, but therein lies a tale. "'Innuendo' started as most things do," Brian told us, "with us just messing around and finding a groove that sounded nice. All of us worked on the arrangement. Freddie started off the theme of the words as he was singing along, then Roger worked on the rest of them. I worked on some of the arrangement, particularly the middle bit, then there was an extra part that Freddie did for the middle as well. It basically came together like a jigsaw puzzle."

shared vocals on 'Tie Your Mother Down' (the ones they could remember, that is!), as well as dipping into his repertoire to perform the *Star Fleet* inmate 'Let Me Out', testing real fans at the Astoria theatre.

In November 1990 Queen had to admit that, yet again, they were going to miss the lucrative Christmas deadline with their new album (one of the problems to beset the band was John's reluctance to actually enter the studio, preferring the comfort of Biarritz). That same month Macbeth opened, with Brian on hand from the first night onwards to supervise the music's integration and chat to various Queen fans who'd come along on the off chance. Also in November *The Sun* claimed "It's official! Freddie is seriously ill", citing an interview with Brian as proof. "It's true that he has been quite rough recently. Freddie is okay and he definitely hasn't got AIDS, but I think his wild rock'n'roll lifestyle has caught up with him. I think he just needs a break." Despite Brian's statement to the contrary, *The Sun* later ran a photograph of Freddie with "top AIDS specialist Dr F Gordon Atkinson", claiming he was suffering from a "mystery illness", as testified by his wizened frame and lifeless mien. The pointed hints were screaming one obvious conclusion, but not even *The Sun* dared say it outright.

Ignoring the rumours, Freddie ploughed himself into his work and the band's new single was released in January. Called 'Innuendo', it was a six and a half minute epic to rival 'Bohemian Rhapsody'.

With a single of such length and stylistic breadth Queen were going out on a limb once more. "It's a very strange track," Brian admitted. "It's a bit of a risk as a single, but it's different and you either win it all or you lose it all." They won it all: 'Innuendo' entered the charts at No 1, breaking the record of 'I Want It All' No 3. It was Queen's second chart topper in their own right, and after five hits had peaked at No 2, you would have been entitled to bet against it happening.

Hollywood Records decided against taking such a risk with their first release, opting instead for the more immediate rocker 'Headlong'. That meant another video, of course. The media jackals had taken the fact that Innuendo's promo film comprised cartoon assemblages of the band to mean that Fred was too ravaged by disease to appear; it was a neat theory, but one shown to be totally without foundation when he joined the rest of the band to record a video for 'Headlong' and two other songs.

Two tracks aired, two instant classics. For a band said to be fighting disease, divorce and disintegration Queen looked like coming up with their best work in years. When the album followed on 4 February it confirmed this fact, soaring to No 1 in the UK as it did so (just No 30 in America). Despite the Queen credits, certain songs have discernible lineage. "I was obviously involved heavily in 'Headlong', 'I Can't Live With You' and 'Hitman'," Brian told us, "while 'All God's People' came from Freddie at the same time as the *Barcelona* project. 'The Show Must Go On' came from Roger and John playing the sequence and I started to put things down. At the beginning it was just this chord sequence but I had this strange feeling that it could be somehow important and I got very impassioned and went and beavered away at it. I sat down with Freddie and we decided what the theme should be and wrote the first verse. It's a long story that song, but I always felt it would be important because we were dealing with things that were hard to talk about at the time, but in the world of music you could do it."

A highlight for many was the second single, a Freddie composition entitled 'I'm Going Slightly Mad'. It was in marked contrast to the overblown nature of the first, and delighted all real fans of the eccentric singer. Unfortunately radio listeners were not inspired enough to drag the song beyond the disappointing low 20s chart-wise, despite its dazzling monochrome video featuring Freddie wigged up to the nines, a kettle headed Taylor, penguin impressionist Brian May and court jester Deacon, plus a new B-side track, 'Lost Opportunity'.

The rest of the album continues the eclectic theme that just the first two singles evoke. 'Headlong' and 'I Can't Live With You' are both bouncy rockers, and then Freddie's falsetto ballad 'Don't Try So Hard' reaches parts Queen hadn't reached for years. Roger's rampaging 'Ride The Wild Wind' is perhaps the best single that never was, encapsulating the songwriting and performance chemistry that had made 'Breakthru', 'Ga Ga' and 'Magic' such classics, while the purity of 'These Are The Days Of Our Lives' was obvious to all long before it was plucked for posthumous kudos.

The critics were amazed at the power left in the band and, more specifically, in Freddie's voice, but undeniably he sings better than ever, ranging from sheer power on 'Hitman' to tender falsetto on 'Don't Try So Hard'. Sounds in particular declared it the group's best ever – five stars! – and most other press reports were pretty encouraging. Q said it was "both endearing and enduring", but real credit must go to *The Daily Telegraph* who struck the perfect chord with their analysis that it was "a cross between Led Zeppelin and Kenneth Williams".

Amidst the swirl of Queen activity Brian as usual, found time for a couple of extra diversions. He scored his second No 1 of the year by producing a song called 'The Stonk' for the charity Comic Relief (at last, one of his charity exercises paid off!), and also appeared in the video. Roger made an appearance too, before

joining The Cross in Bath during March for work on their third album (Rufus Tiger Taylor was born to him and Debbie in the same month). In May he was back in Switzerland, however, for hastily reconvened Queen sessions – with Freddie's impetus spurring them forwards, work on the next album, begun in January, continued. Towards the end of May Brian set off on a laborious PR trawl across the States where he played live on radio shows in between denying rumours about Freddie and explaining why the band weren't touring. In his absence the remaining three were filmed miming 'The Days Of Our Lives' for future US single release (Brian's part was filmed later and 'edited' in – spot the join!). Freddie wore a gorgeous cat embroidered waistcoat, but hardly anyone noticed; they were looking at the gaunt face and the sunken cheeks. Only the gleam in his eyes gave any indication that it was the same man who had strutted his way through the 26 date European tour.

In America Hollywood Records lived up to its promise of relaunching Queen with production of a documentary called Days Of Our Lives. It was basically a condensed version of 'The Magic Years', but brought up to date and featuring a voiceover scripted and read by Guns N' Roses main man W Axl Rose, self confessed Queen addict. Hollywood had also begun remastering and re-

Picture on opposite page: **"This tour will be bigger than bigness itself. It will make Ben Hur look like The Muppets" – Roger**

Picture above: **John and Roger completed an amazing 112 interviews in 16 days for The Works**

releasing the back catalogue they had gone to such lengths to acquire. On top of just improving upon EMI's appalling job of converting the lot onto CD, Hollywood drafted in various big shot remixers to do their worst on a couple of tracks on each album. The exercise threw up some great moments – Rick Rubin's fantastic reworking of 'We Will Rock You' and Freddy Bastone's daring dance mix of 'Seven Seas Of Rhye', for example – while other songs like 'Stone Cold Crazy', 'Body Language' and 'You're My Best Friend' are just tidied up to the extent that only professional sound engineers can spot the difference. Rare edits of 'Keep Yourself Alive' and 'Liar' are included on *Queen*, alongside an unearthed track left over from those first sessions called 'Mad The Swine' (used in the UK as Headlong's B-side).

Solo projects again materialised in 1991, with The Cross's excellent new single, 'New Dark Ages', once again going largely unbought. Brian openly aired a solo track – 'Lost Horizon' – on the Richard Digance television show, while smuggling another – 'Driven By You' – into the public consciousness by allowing it to become the jingle for a high profile Ford car advertisement. In October he acted as musical director at a huge guitar festival in Seville called Expo 92, where he played with a host of other major six string slingers, including Steve Vai, Joe Satriani, Nuno Bettencourt and Joe Walsh. Other guests included Paul Rodgers, Cozy Powell, Neil Murray, Rick Wakeman and Nathan East.

Back in England Queen released their fourth single from the multi-platinum *Innuendo*. 'The Show Must Go On' was never allowed the courtesy of being judged as just another Queen song. Everyone who heard it interpreted the lyric as virtually Fred's epitaph, or certainly the closing chapter of his life. Matters weren't helped by the fact that the song's video featured no new footage, just clips of past glories pasted together. The question had to be asked: was Freddie too ill to appear?

Picture: **"I read somewhere – in Rolling Stone, I think – that John Lennon heard 'Crazy Little Thing Called Love' and it gave him the impetus to start recording again"** *– Roger*

On 28 October 1991, *Greatest Hits II* was released to phenomenal response. Two No 1s, a No 2, three No 3s... Hardly anyone could resist its obvious charms and in just two months it became the year's third best selling album (they'd made the Christmas deadline for once). As had happened 10 years earlier, the album was accompanied by Greatest Flix II and Greatest Pix II, which again topped their respective charts. A double video package called Box Of Flix combined both Flix sets with four unavailable clips from the early days and was only held off the pinnacle of the video charts by Flix II.

Sales would have been high anyway, but the events of November meant that no other record stood a chance. On 23 November, Freddie gave permission for the following statement to be released to the press: "Following the enormous conjecture in the press over the last two weeks, I wish to confirm that I have been tested HIV positive and have AIDS. I felt it correct to keep this information private to protect the privacy of those around me. However, the time has now come for my friends and fans around the world to know the truth, and I hope that everyone will join with me, my doctors and all those worldwide in the fight against this terrible disease."

Just 24 hours later, while the announcement was still screaming from the front pages of all the Sunday papers, Freddie Mercury died.

To a world that had perhaps begun to suspect the truth, although still desperately hoping against it, the news came as an almighty shock. Even the previous day's press release hadn't prepared anyone.

Freddie died at 7:00pm British time, but his death wasn't announced until midnight's press release: "Freddie Mercury died peacefully this evening at his home in Kensington, London. His death was the result of bronchial pneumonia, brought on by AIDS." For most people, the news came during breakfast on Monday. Early morning television and radio were buzzing with the announcement, each drafting in their own panels of so called experts to put his life, work and, now, death into perspective. The newspapers were all thrown off guard by the suddenness of it all, and many first editions slipped out containing stories with such anachronistic banners as "Parents In Bedside Vigil" and "Freddie Has Hours To Live". The second editions were a different matter. "AIDS Kills The King Of Rock" ran *The Daily Star*; "Rock Star Freddie Is Dead" said *The Daily Mirror*; "Mercury Loses His AIDS Fight" *The Daily Mail* printed; "Queen Star Freddie Dies" was *The Daily Express*'s comment.

After the initial business of breaking the news, several publications settled on a policy of condemnation, blaming Freddie for his own death. Such anti-homosexual jingoism could have worked with any other person, but Freddie's sexuality was a tiny aspect of his life – millions loved him for who he was, not what he was – and the overwhelming level of public support for him caused the papers to change their stance.

Tributes poured into the Queen office and Freddie's home from friends, colleagues and fans, both past and present. No words could convey the true depth of anyone's feelings, but the attempt that comes closest originated from Queen themselves: "We have lost the greatest and most beloved member of our family. We feel overwhelming grief that he has gone, sadness that he should be cut down at the height of his creativity, but above all great pride in the courageous way that he lived and died. It has been a privilege for us to have shared such magical times. As soon as we are able we would like to celebrate his life in the style to which he was accustomed."

Tributes continued to flood in. On the Monday evening the BBC screened a touching, if hastily assembled, programme on his life, introduced by an obviously distraught Elton John. Flowers arrived by the van load at Fred's Logan Place address, and all had to be ferried into the grounds. On the Tuesday night Freddie's staff, Feebie, Joe and Terry, still in shock themselves, opened the gates to Garden Lodge and invited in the weeping mass of fans outside to see the amazing floral carpet of bouquets resting gently under the stunning Christmas tree. It was a touching gesture, one befitting such a generous spirit as Freddie Mercury.

His cremation took place on 27 November at the West London Crematorium. It was a strictly private affair, but of the few friends and relatives present, probably only Bomi and Jer Bulsara understood much of the ceremony as it was conducted in keeping with their Zoroastrian faith. The music of Montserrat Caballé was played as the mourners made their way outside the hall.

While Freddie's millions of fans wept far away, unable to do anything to help, someone was thinking of them. Characteristically Brian used his own time of grieving to reach out to those others he felt were being ignored: the fans. On the night of the cremation, he sat down and wrote the following words to be published in the Queen Fan Club's Official Magazine: "As you by now know, Freddie was fighting the terrible AIDS disease for many years, and for much of the time even we didn't know. For Freddie, his art and his friends were everything – he poured himself with huge vigour into both. He was determined that no hint of frailty should mar his music, or our music, or make life difficult for his friends. By refusing to concede anything to the illness, his amazing strength and courage enabled him to continue at full strength in making albums, videos, etc, even though it cost him more and more in private pain. He never in our hearing complained about his lot, and never let despondency creep into his work, his voice seemed to get miraculously better and better. And he died without ever losing control.

"Freddie never wanted sympathy, he wanted exactly what the fans gave him – belief, support and the endorsement of that strangely winding road to excellence that we, Queen, have tried to follow. You gave him support in being the outstandingly free spirit that he was, and is. Freddie, his music, his dazzling creative energy – those are for ever."

Freddie was gone. While he had been alive the press proliferated rumours to the effect he was dying. Now their pages were filled with trying to piece together his remaining minutes, hours, days and months. Slowly parts of the painful truth emerged. Mary Austin, who had been by Freddie's bedside for most of his final days, sadly missed his passing by 10 minutes when she popped out on an errand. Dave Clarke did share the moment (Jim Hutton later touchingly recalled Freddie's last words as "pee pee", the pair's abbreviation for needing to go to the toilet).

With hindsight, much of Freddie's last work can be reappraised. Even in the last videos, he maintained his poise, his posturing and

Main picture: *"I like people to go away from a Queen show feeling fully entertained. I think Queen songs are pure escapism, like going to see a good film"*

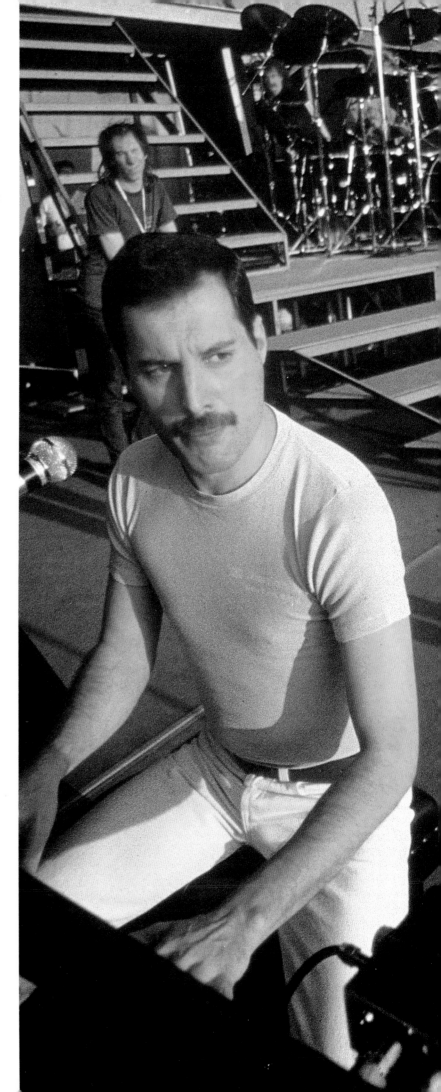

his decorum. A rare film of outtakes from the recording of 'I'm Going Slightly Mad' shows him physically weak, facially gaunt, but mentally in control. No detail is ignored or overlooked. John is instructed where to sit; Roger has a lesson in how best to throttle the bewigged singer; Brian is directed on how to move his fingers; even a penguin's movements are scripted by the increasingly worn Mercury. His industry masked a severely worsening condition and the need for a bed on set for rest between takes. Similarly during filming for 'Days Of Our Lives' Freddie triumphed against the most acute pain to get his performance done. Despite having to recuperate on a nearby stool after every couple of lines, he persevered with customary determination.

Freddie's final video would be his epitaph yet. Together with 'Bohemian Rhapsody', 'These Are The Days Of Our Lives' was released as a double A-sided single in aid of the Terrence Higgins Trust, Freddie's stipulated charity. The record was pressed and released in a week and entered the UK charts at No 1 where it stayed for five weeks, making 'Bohemian Rhapsody' the only song to hit No 1 twice (and at Christmas again), and the UK's best selling single ever. In December another record was broken as 10 of Queen's albums were to be found in the UK Top 100; people couldn't get enough of Freddie's voice.

Within days of Freddie's death Brian's TV jingle, 'Driven By You', was finally released as a single. As the release date approached he realised that Freddie's time was limited and considered pulling the record. However, when Brian's fears were relayed to Freddie he dismissed them out of hand, replying "Tell him he must release it. What better publicity could he have?" The song reached No 6.

A year after their last success there, 12 February saw the BPI awards honour Queen and Freddie with a special trophy. They were also presented with the award for Best Selling Single of the previous year, the 'Bo Rap/Days Of Our Lives' double whammy. Roger and Brian collected the honours in Fred's name and also used the fact that the show was being broadcast live to announce a very special tribute show to be held at Wembley on 20 April, with tickets going on sale the following day.

All 72,000 tickets for the Freddie Mercury Tribute Concert For AIDS Awareness sold out in six hours, and that was before any names had been announced as playing. All would be revealed...

When the big day – a British Bank Holiday Monday – arrived the sun shone after a downcast weekend. Crowds had gathered the night before, desperate for a good position inside the packed stadium. The show officially started at 6:00pm with Roger, John and Brian taking to the stage to provide the official welcome. Brian announced that they were there to honour "the life and work and dreams of one Freddie Mercury" while Roger encouraged people to "cry as much as you like". For John it was quite possibly the most nerve-wracking moment of his life; having hardly – if ever – spoken on stage, he now had to address 72,000 people in the stadium plus the estimated half a billion watching worldwide via satellite. Cheered on by the gestures of Brian and Roger he announced the arrival of Metallica – the concert had begun.

After James Hetfield's group had run through three of their own hits, Extreme attempted an ambitious medley of Queen material to wonderful applause. Def Leppard (joined by "the man with the curly hair and the curly guitar lead") followed, plus Bob Geldof, Spinal Tap (really!) and Guns N' Roses who for many stole the show. Most people were surprised at the LA band's appearance given Axl's previous homophobic statements, and some degree of demonstration within the audience was experienced. A close look at the video of the day reveals Axl yelling "Shove it" during the opening chorus of 'Paradise City'. Far from being a tribute to The Cross's first album, he was actually pointing to a banner (off screen) which bore the words "Piss off Axl". Approximately two seconds after his yell, the banner mysteriously disappeared...

The first half of the show also featured live link ups with South Africa and a recording of U2 from the previous night, and it was closed by a speech from Elizabeth Taylor. Then came the moment everyone had been waiting for. A recording of Freddie's "This is what you wanted, this is what you're gonna get" was suddenly played before explosions and smoke bombs announced the remainder of Queen were on stage, together at last. They began with 'Tie Your Mother Down', Brian on vocals until he was relieved by Joe Elliott. With Roger, John, Brian and Spike the main players, an endless procession of singers trouped on to pay homage to Freddie. Robert Plant, one of Freddie's biggest influences, picked his way through 'Innuendo' then 'Crazy Little Thing Called Love'; Roger Daltrey tackled 'I Want It All' while Paul Young chose 'Radio Ga Ga'. Things got very special when David Bowie performed 'Under Pressure' with Annie Lennox taking Fred's role; Bowie then introduced Ian Hunter and Mick Ronson before the three of them turned in one of the performances of the night, a blistering 'All The Young Dudes'; Bowie's next rendition, of the Lord's Prayer, was less expected (as he left the stage he yelled, "Follow that!").

Boyhood Queen fan George Michael had been eagerly awaited and when he arrived to sing 'Days Of Our Lives' with Lisa

Stansfield he didn't disappoint. He even recreated a touch of the Queen of old with a burst of '39' before soaring through a spotless version of 'Somebody To Love'. Next Elton John appeared unannounced and sporting a newly adorned 'hair weave', to run through the opening sections of 'Bohemian Rhapsody'. The opera part was played on tape as usual, then for the heavy metal middle Axl Rose exploded onto the stage before joining Elton for the song's more sedate climax. Yet another remarkable teaming, made for the spirit of Freddie.

Elton belted out his version of 'The Show Must Go On' before Axl returned (in his third costume) for 'We Will Rock You'. But there could only be one finale and, according to Brian, one person to sing it: in the show's most surprising moment yet, Freddie's long time idol, Liza Minnelli walked out to perform 'We Are The Champions' with her usual style. The rest of the day's acts filtered on behind her (Elton aside; he was too upset) to create one of the most memorable moments in stadium rock: 'Guns N' Roses' backing a woman usually accompanied by Frank Sinatra. Whatever her credentials, Liza's parting call was heartfelt: "Thank you, Freddie. We just wanted to let you know we were thinking of you!"

Tears flowed, hearts ached and, for all the nonsense of it, more than one person half expected Freddie himself to walk out at the end. But it couldn't happen. Not thanks to AIDS. Freddie was gone for good but he left a wonderful body of work as his legacy and, if any tribute needed to be paid to his talent it is this: George Michael may have sung 'Somebody To Love' brilliantly and James Hetfield had got gruff enough to do 'Stone Cold Crazy' justice and Axl had just about handled 'Bo Rap's' metal act, but could they have swapped songs? It's unlikely. More than a dozen different singers had been needed to fill the shoes of one man. That's some achievement for anyone.

Picture: **"This is what you wanted, this is what you're gonna get!"**

EPILOGUE
The Show Must Go On

Queen ended officially on 20 April 1992, but still there was work to be done. The Freddie Mercury Tribute raised more than £10,000,000 for AIDS charities. 'Bohemian Rhapsody' had already earned £1,000,000 for the Terrence Higgins Trust, but now a new charity called the Mercury Phoenix Trust was set up to focus the work in Freddie's name. 'Bohemian Rhapsody's' fund raising didn't stop in England; its use in the hit film Wayne's World combined with the effects of the Tribute sparked interest in America where it soared to No 2 – proceeds going to the Magic Johnson AIDS Foundation. The US version of *Hits II*, *Classic Queen*, reached No 4 – their best position for more than a decade.

26 May saw the release of a new Queen album: *Live At Wembley 86*. It wasn't exactly new, but it was complete unlike that aural monstrosity *Live Magic*; fans could hear every off note, every missed harmony, every expletive – oh, and every song of their brilliant set, including the rock'n'roll medley and 'Big Spender'. It reached No 2.

Another Queen album arrived soon after but it wasn't eligible to chart. Included as part of a lavish Box Of Tricks it was called *The 12" Collection* and boasted every single which had been put out in an extended form. It was far from complete: 'Keep Passing The Open Windows', 'Back Chat', 'One Vision' and 'Scandal' were all absent while for some reason 'Bohemian Rhapsody' and 'The Show Must Go On' were included. The 'Box' also contained a colourful poster, badge, glossy book and rare video of Queen Live At The Rainbow and was available through mail order only. One for the fans.

That summer saw Freddie back in the charts. The Olympics had finally come to town in Barcelona, and to commemorate they dropped Freddie and Montserrat's famous tribute. Not to worry, the BBC still used it as its official coverage theme, prompting a worthy re-release and a healthy stay very near the top of the charts.

November 92 saw Freddie back again with a new Christmas single and album. 'In My Defence' was one of the songs he'd recorded for the musical Time, but as part of a remix campaign it was released to ravenous response and was soon buzzing around the Top 5. The record from which it came, *The Freddie Mercury Album*, featured a selection of his best songs reworked. The jury went out on its success for some time before returning a thumbs up verdict. Highlights included the beefier 'Love Kills' and ' Living On My Own'. It was also the first time 'The Great Pretender' had appeared on an album/CD.

Brian was being no slouch himself that year. In fact, work was the only way he could keep his mind off the hurt he was still feeling. The Tribute Concert had seen him perform a solo track called 'Too Much Love Will Kill You' with just Spike for accompaniment. At the time he offered it as the best he had; by summer he was ready to air it properly as a single and it promptly hit No 5, one place higher than 'Driven By You'. On 21 September, after five years in the making, *Back To The Light*, Brian's début album (the mini LP aside) was ready for public consumption, that too scoring a healthy No 6 in the UK. Highlights were the singles, the moody 'The Dark' (first tested for Macbeth) and the barnstorming 'Resurrection' which had originally started out as an instrumental track on Cozy Powell's *The Drums Are Back* album. The title track reached No 19 as a

Main picture (right):
The official attendance at Knebworth was 120,000, but police estimates suggested double that

single in November, almost certainly bought for the B-sides (over its two CD release, Brian insisted on including the whole of the *Star Fleet Project* – it had made it onto CD at last). A tour was threatened but English fans would have to wait; Brian wasn't about to try anything at home that he hadn't well and truly tested elsewhere.

Brian also found time to pop up alongside Elton John for a Wembley re-run of 'The Show Must Go On' from earlier in the year, as well as appearing on Bert Weedon's *This Is Your Life* and helping out on his idol Hank Marvin's latest album. Hank wanted to do his bit for AIDS research and so with Brian recorded a charity version of 'We Are The Champions'. Roger too kept busy, even contributing some drums on Shakin' Stevens' hit 'Radio'.

The guest sessions continued into the new year for Brian. Paul Rodgers, Gordon Giltrap and Dweezil Zappa were this year's lucky recipients of the Red Special touch. The result on Paul's version of 'I'm Ready' perhaps suggests why Brian has rarely tried blues, but Paul was happy; as was Gordon when Brian added to

his classic instrumental 'Heartsong': "I would have settled for some three part harmony playing but he gave me four part!" For Dweezil Brian had to play "like Brian May – he wanted personality more than anything", but as yet the results remain unheard.

During some support shows in South America Brian felt quite uneasy for the first few gigs before acquiring his stage legs. "I was nervous," he readily admits. "The first three were quite awkward. I didn't know when I was supposed to be singing or playing at any one time, and combining the two was quite difficult. But for number four we were in Velez Sarsfield, in the same stadium Queen used to play. I was supporting Joe Cocker and something happened. The audience were incredibly up and pleased to see us."

Audiences continued to be "up" in North America where this time The Brian May Band – Jamie Moses, Spike, Cozy, Neil Murray, Cathy Porter and Shelley Preston – supported Guns N' Roses. It was as much a thrill for Axl and co to have Brian along, so the tour went well for all, with Slash joining The BM Band on The Tonight Show in New York, and both bands hitting the stage in Paris to sing 'Knockin' On Heaven's Door'.

In Britain there could be no band big enough to headline over Brian and, duly inspired, he began his first UK tour to marvellous responses. From Edinburgh to Whitley Bay to Birmingham to Cardiff to London, he was lauded like nowhere else in the world. His choice of mixing the new material with Queen classics like 'Tie Your Mother Down' and 'Hammer To Fall' couldn't fail to please; the only risk he took was choosing to perform Freddie's trademark, 'Love Of My Life'. He needn't have fretted; night after night, emotional audiences carried him through. As a note for the future, encores usually ended with Brian's own lyric to John Lennon's 'God', featuring the savage line "I don't believe in Queen/I just believe in me".

A new single, 'Resurrection', released to coincide with the tour spent limited time inside the Top 40. With George Michael's help Queen reached No 1 with the Tribute version of 'Someone To Love', but once again the summer's high scorer from the band would be their late singer. August saw the release of yet another remix of Fred's solo track 'Living On My Own' throughout Europe. In the UK it captured the spirit of summer and leapt straight to No 1, becoming the biggest solo success of any member yet. *The Freddie Mercury Album* received a new lease of life, even though its version of the song was quite different.

After another stint abroad, the Brian May circus arrived back in the UK in December for its final European leg. The visit included a remarkable night at the Royal Albert Hall, where Brian overcame flu to perform. For this tour, 'Teo Torriatte' became the encore and 'Lost Horizon' the accompanying single. The live impetus was maintained in 1994 by the February release of the album *Live At The Brixton Academy*. On the plus side it gave a real flavour of what BM gets up to when left to his own devices; on the other hand, stage talk is minimal (and he is so good at it) and songs like 'Resurrection' and 'Love Of My Life', appallingly cocked up on the night, appear to have undergone severe re-recording in the studio.

Also in February Brian made a high profile appearance alongside his great pals Bon Jovi at the annual BPI (or Brit) awards. It was not to be his last guest spot of the year, also turning out for the Gibson Guitar Company's Night Of 100 Guitars (when he was the only guitarist present not playing a Gibson) and with Meat Loaf at Wembley in December (for some good old rock'n'roll and a couple of blasts of 'We Will Rock You'). He was busy, even masquerading as dead country star Conway Twitty (or "Twit Conway") at a Fan Club party, but really the year belonged to Roger.

After some soul searching, Roger finally had to disband The Cross. Despite their third album, *Blue Rock*, being quite excellent, it had again failed to sell. Now he would have a go with another solo album, but this time under his own name. The first result came in May with the controversially titled *Nazis 1994*. It was by no means a right wing record, in fact it attacked outright the idea of fascism, yet it was misinterpreted and banned by Radio One in the UK. It did however spend one week at No 22 – the highest position of Roger's career – despite poor reviews: "Roger Taylor's heart may be in the right place, but sadly his musical taste is well up his arse" wrote *Kerrang*.

The following album, *Happiness?*, fared little better reviews-wise: *NME* summed up its slating with the words "What a berk", while *Kerrang* confined itself to the conclusion that "*Happiness?* is nowhere near as bad as we might have expected". The album's content was yet another change of style for Roger, centring more on the rhythmic influences behind his 'Days Of Our Lives' than 'Blue Rock''s bluster. Controversy continued with the scathing 'Dear Mr Murdoch', but there was no escaping the emotion on 'Old Friend' – pure love for Freddie.

In autumn Roger embarked on his first ever solo tour, kicking off with a superb gig at the Shepherd's Bush Empire. Keen use of back drops and photos were made throughout, most efficiently on 'Old Friend' and 'Nazis'. The presence of 'Ride The Wild Wind' and 'I Want To Break Free' kept the Queen fans happy, but Roger deserved the success in his own right with his best album yet. A Japanese tour followed the date, before the band returned to the UK for more gigs – although sadly without the screens this time around.

The tour and album and even his role in the 'Who Is The Real Peter Green?' confusion kept Roger in the news, while Brian busied himself with presenting *Kerrang* awards, going to Disney premieres and recording the themes to Radio One's *Spider Man* series and ITV's Frank Stubbs. (One TV critic had this to say: "And the less said about Brian May's new soundtrack the better.")

The Queen solo careers seem to be taking care of themselves, and for the most part fans happily divide their time between Brian and Roger's activities (sadly John seems content with his low profile). But the one topic that none of them can avoid being asked concerns new material: is there any?

The answer is yes, and it will hopefully be released before Christmas 1995 (assuming the deadline jinx doesn't strike again). Between working on solo projects or just resting, the three remaining members have all been hard at work sorting through the untouched legacy, trying to figure out what can be released. There are several options. For one, Brian admits that Freddie put down vocals to at least four songs in those final recording sessions; the band now hope to finish the tracks around his voice. Then there is the version of 'Too Much Love Will Kill You' recorded by Queen for inclusion on *The Miracle*; that will almost certainly find its way onto a new album. Tracks like 'Heaven For Everyone' which already feature Fred's voice are good candidates for a reworking, and finally there are new songs with vocals from Roger or Brian.

The possibilities are many, but only one thing is certain; nothing will be released if it in any way spoils Fred's memory. Standards haven't slipped with his passing as Brian is sure to appreciate given his recent experiences. "I have this sense that Freddie is standing behind my shoulder in the studio," he admitted in March 1995. "He didn't realise he would last so long and was recording up to his death. After listening to Freddie's voice for so long it's as if he is with me. I want to turn round and say, Hey what do you think of that? Queen fans will not be disappointed. There's some good stuff."

With the band set to work together publicly one last time, all the tribulations littering their history are forgotten. Queen have been supposedly on the brink of splitting up since 1973 according to various press reports. But they knew they had more to offer as a band than as four individuals and spent the next two decades proving it. On 12 July 1986, at Wembley Stadium in front of an audience of 72,000 fans Freddie Mercury had declared: "We're gonna stay together until we fucking well die."

And they did.

Albums (UK)

Queen
EMI EMC 3006
Released 13 July 1973. Reached No 24

Keep Yourself Alive (May), Doing All Right (May/Staffell), Great King Rat (Mercury), My Fairy King (Mercury), Liar (Mercury), The Night Comes Down (May), Modern Times Rock'N'Roll (Taylor), Son And Daughter (May), Jesus (Mercury), Seven Seas Of Rhye (Mercury).

Queen II
EMI EMA 767
Released 8 March 1974. Reached No 5

Side White: Procession (May), Father To Son (May), White Queen (As It Began) (May), Some Day One Day (May), The Loser In The End (Taylor); Side Black: Ogre Battle (Mercury), The Fairy Feller's Master Stroke (Mercury), Nevermore (Mercury), The March Of The Black Queen (Mercury), Funny How Love Is (Mercury), Seven Seas Of Rhye (Mercury).

Sheer Heart Attack
EMI EMC 3061
Released 8 November 1974. Reached No 2

Brighton Rock (May), Killer Queen (Mercury), Tenement Funster (Taylor), Flick Of The Wrist (Mercury), Lily Of The Valley (Mercury), Now I'm Here (May), In The Lap Of The Gods (Mercury), Stone Cold Crazy (May/Mercury/Taylor/Deacon), Dear Friends (May), Misfire (Deacon), Bring Back That Leroy Brown (Mercury), She Makes Me (Stormtrooper In Stilettos) (May), In The Lap Of The Gods... Revisited (Mercury).

A Night At The Opera
EMI EMTC 103
Released 21 November 1975. Reached No 1

Death On Two Legs (Dedicated To...) (Mercury), Lazing On A Sunday Afternoon (Mercury), I'm In Love With My Car (Taylor), 39 (May), You're My Best Friend (Deacon), Sweet Lady (May), Seaside Rendezvous (Mercury), The Prophet's Song (May), Love Of My Life (Mercury), Good Company (May), Bohemian Rhapsody (Mercury), God Save The Queen (Trad Arr May).

A Day At The Races
EMI EMTC 104
Released 10 December 1976. Reached No 1

Tie Your Mother Down (May), You Take My Breath Away (Mercury), Long Away (May), The Millionaire Waltz (Mercury), You And I (Deacon), Somebody To Love (Mercury), White Man (May), Good Old Fashioned Lover Boy (Mercury), Drowse (Taylor), Teo Torriatte (Let Us Cling Together) (May).

News Of The World
EMI EMA 784
Released 28 October 1977. Reached No 4

We Will Rock You (May), We Are The Champions (Mercury), Sheer Heart Attack (Taylor), All Dead All Dead (May), Spread Your Wings (Deacon), Fight From The Inside (Taylor), Get Down Make Love (Mercury), Sleeping On The Sidewalk (May), Who Needs You (Deacon), It's Late (May), My Melancholy Blues (Mercury).

Jazz
EMI EMA 788
Released 10 November 1978. Reached No 2

Mustapha (Mercury), Fat Bottomed Girls (May), Jealousy (Mercury), Bicycle Race (Mercury), If You Can't Beat Them (Deacon), Let Me Entertain You (Mercury), Dead On Time (May), In Only Seven Days (Deacon), Dreamers Ball (May), Fun It (Taylor), Leaving Home Ain't Easy (May), Don't Stop Me Now (Mercury), More Of That Jazz (Taylor).

Live Killers
EMI EMSP 330
Released 22 June 1979. Reached No 3

We Will Rock You (May), Let Me Entertain You (Mercury), Death On Two Legs (Dedicated To...) (Mercury), Killer Queen (Mercury), Bicycle Race (Mercury), I'm In Love With My Car (Taylor), Get Down Make Love (Mercury), You're My Best Friend (Deacon), Now I'm Here (May), Dreamers Ball (May), Love Of My Life (Mercury), 39 (May), Keep Yourself Alive (May), Don't Stop Me Now (Mercury), Spread Your Wings (Deacon), Brighton Rock (May), Mustapha (Mercury), Bohemian Rhapsody (Mercury), Tie Your Mother Down (May), Sheer Heart Attack (Taylor), We Will Rock You (May), We Are The Champions (Mercury), God Save The Queen (Trad Arr May).

The Game
EMI EMA 795
Released 30 June 1980. Reached No 1

Play The Game (Mercury), Dragon Attack (May), Another One Bites The Dust (Deacon), Need Your Loving Tonight (Deacon), Crazy Little Thing Called Love (Mercury), Rock It (Prime Jive) (Taylor), Don't Try Suicide (Mercury), Sail Away Sweet Sister (May), Coming Soon (Taylor), Save Me (May).

Flash Gordon (Original Soundtrack)
EMI EMC 3351
Released 8 December 1980. Reached No 10

Flash's Theme (May), In The Space Capsule (The Love Theme) (Taylor), Ming's Theme (In The Court Of Ming The Merciless) (Mercury), The Ring (Hypnotic Seduction Of Dale) (Mercury), Football Fight (Mercury), In The Death Cell (Love Theme

Reprise) (Taylor), Execution Of Flash (Deacon), The Kiss (Aura Resurrects Flash) (Mercury), Arboria (Planet Of The Tree Men) (Deacon), Escape From The Swamp (Taylor), Flash To The Rescue (May), Vultan's Theme (Attack Of The Hawk Men) (Mercury), Battle Theme (May), The Wedding March (Trad Arr May), Marriage Of Dale And Ming (And Flash Approaching) (May/Taylor), Crash Dive On Mingo City (May), Flash's Theme Reprise (Victory Celebrations) (May), The Hero (May).

Greatest Hits
EMI EMTV 30
Released 2 November 1981. Reached No 1

Bohemian Rhapsody (Mercury), Another One Bites The Dust (Deacon), Killer Queen (Mercury), Fat Bottomed Girls (May), Bicycle Race (Mercury), You're My Best Friend (Deacon), Don't Stop Me Now (Mercury), Save Me (May), Crazy Little Thing Called Love (Mercury), Somebody To Love (Mercury), Now I'm Here (May), Good Old Fashioned Lover Boy (Mercury), Play The Game (Mercury), Flash (May), Seven Seas Of Rhye (Mercury), We Will Rock You (May), We Are The Champions (Mercury).

Hot Space
EMI EMA 797
Released 21 May 1982. Reached No 4

Staying Power (Mercury), Dancer (May), Back Chat (Deacon), Body Language (Mercury), Action This Day (Taylor), Put Out The Fire (May), Life Is Real (Song For Lennon) (Mercury), Calling All Girls (Taylor), Las Palabras De Amor (The Words Of Love) (May), Cool Cat (Mercury/Deacon), Under Pressure (Queen/Bowie).

The Works
EMI EMC 2400141
Released 27 February 1984. Reached No 2

Radio Ga Ga (Taylor), Tear It Up (May), It's A Hard Life (Mercury), Man On The Prowl (Mercury), Machines (Or Back To Humans) (Taylor/May), I Want To Break Free (Deacon), Keep Passing The Open Windows (Mercury), Hammer To Fall (May), Is This The World We Created? (Mercury/May).

The Complete Works
EMI QB1
Released 2 December 1985

Complete Vision See What A Fool I've Been (May), A Human Body (Taylor), Soul Brother (Queen), I Go Crazy (May), Thank God It's Christmas (Taylor/May), One Vision (Queen), Blurred Vision (Queen).

A Kind Of Magic
EMI EU 3509

Released 2 June 1986. Reached No 1

One Vision (Queen), A Kind Of Magic (Taylor), One Year Of Love (Deacon), Pain Is So Close To Pleasure (Mercury/Deacon), Friends Will Be Friends (Mercury/Deacon), Who Wants To Live Forever (May), Gimme The Prize (Kurgan's Theme) (May), Don't Lose Your Head (Taylor), Princes Of The Universe (Mercury).

Live Magic
EMI EMC 3519
Released 1 December 1986. Reached No 3

One Vision (Queen), Tie Your Mother Down (May), Seven Seas Of Rhye (Mercury), A Kind Of Magic (Taylor), Under Pressure (Queen/Bowie), Another One Bites The Dust (Deacon), I Want To Break Free (Deacon), Is This The World We Created? (Mercury/May), Bohemian Rhapsody (Mercury), Hammer To Fall (May), Radio Ga Ga (Taylor), We Will Rock You (May), Friends Will Be Friends (Mercury/Deacon), We Are The Champions (Mercury), God Save The Queen (Trad Arr May).

The Miracle
Parlophone PCSD 107
Released 22 May 1989. Reached No 1

Party (Queen), Khashoggi's Ship (Queen), The Miracle (Queen), I Want It All (Queen), The Invisible Man (Queen), Breakthru (Queen), Rain Must Fall (Queen), Scandal (Queen), My Baby Does Me (Queen), Was It All Worth It (Queen).

Queen At The Beeb
Band Of Joy BOJ 001
Released 4 December 1989. Reached No 67

My Fairy King (Mercury), Keep Yourself Alive (May), Doing All Right (May/Staffell), Liar (Mercury), Ogre Battle (Mercury), Great King Rat (Mercury), Modern Times Rock'N'Roll (Taylor), Son And Daughter (May).

Innuendo
Parlophone PCSD 115
Released 4 February 1991. Reached No 1

Innuendo (Queen), I'm Going Slightly Mad (Queen), Headlong (Queen), I Can't Live With You (Queen), Don't Try So Hard (Queen), Ride The Wild Wind (Queen), All God's People (Queen/Moran), These Are The Days Of Our Lives (Queen), Delilah (Queen), The Hitman (Queen), Bijou (Queen), The Show Must Go On (Queen).

Greatest Hits II
Parlophone PMTV 2
Released 28 October 1991. Reached No 1

A Kind Of Magic (Taylor), Under Pressure (Queen/Bowie),

Radio Ga Ga (Taylor), I Want It All (Queen), I Want To Break Free (Deacon), Innuendo (Queen), It's A Hard Life (Mercury), Breakthru (Queen), Who Wants To Live Forever (May), Headlong (Queen), The Miracle (Queen), I'm Going Slightly Mad (Queen), The Invisible Man (Queen), Hammer To Fall (May), Friends Will Be Friends (Mercury/Deacon), The Show Must Go On (Queen), One Vision (Queen).

Queen 12" Remixes
Parlophone CDQTEL 0001

Bohemian Rhapsody (Mercury), Radio Ga Ga (Taylor), Machines (Or Back To Humans) (Taylor/May), I Want To Break Free (Deacon), It's A Hard Life (Mercury), Hammer To Fall (May), Man On The Prowl (Mercury), A Kind Of Magic (Taylor), Pain Is So Close To Pleasure (Mercury/Deacon), Breakthru (Queen), The Invisible Man (Queen), The Show Must Go On (Queen).

Live At Wembley 86
Parlophone 7 99594 2
Released 26 May 1992. Reached No 2

One Vision (Queen), Tie Your Mother Down (May), In The Lap Of The Gods... Revisited (Mercury), Seven Seas Of Rhye (Mercury), Tear It Up (May), A Kind Of Magic (Taylor), Under Pressure (Queen/Bowie), Another One Bites The Dust (Deacon), Who Wants To Live Forever (May), I Want To Break Free (Deacon), Brighton Rock (May), Now I'm Here (May), Love Of My Life (Mercury), Is This The World We Created? (Mercury/May), (You're So Square) Baby I Don't Care (Lieber/Stoller), Hello Mary Lou (Pitney), Tutti Frutti (Penniman/LaBostrie), Gimme Some Lovin' (Winwood/Winwood/Davis), Bohemian Rhapsody (Mercury), Hammer To Fall (May), Crazy Little Thing Called Love (Mercury), Big Spender (Coleman/Fields), Radio Ga Ga (Taylor), We Will Rock You (May), Friends Will Be Friends (Mercury/Deacon), We Are The Champions (Mercury), God Save The Queen (Trad Arr May).

Singles (UK)

Keep Yourself Alive/Son And Daughter
EMI 2036. Released 6 July 1973. Failed to chart

Seven Seas Of Rhye/See What A Fool I've Been
EMI 2121. Released 23 February 1974. Reached No 10

Killer Queen/Flick Of The Wrist (double A-side)
EMI 2229. Released 11 October 1974. Reached No 2

Now I'm Here/Lily Of The Valley
EMI 2256. Released 17 January 1975. Reached No 11

Bohemian Rhapsody/I'm In Love With My Car
EMI 2375. Released 31 October 1975. Reached No 1

You're My Best Friend/39
EMI 2494. Released 18 June 1976. Reached No 7

Somebody To Love/White Man
EMI 2565. Released 12 November 1976. Reached No 2

Tie Your Mother Down/You And I
EMI 2593. Released 4 March 1977. Reached No 31

Queen's First EP: Good Old Fashioned Lover Boy/Death On Two Legs (Dedicated To...)/Tenement Funster/White Queen (As It Began)
EMI 2623. Released 20 May 1977. Reached No 17

We Are The Champions/We Will Rock You
EMI 2708. Released 7 October 1977. Reached No 2

Spread Your Wings/Sheer Heart Attack
EMI 2757. Released 10 February 1978. Reached No 34

Fat Bottomed Girls/Bicycle Race (double A-side)
EMI 2870. Released 13 October 1978. Reached No 11

Don't Stop Me Now/In Only Seven Days
EMI 2910. Released 26 January 1979. Reached No 9

Love Of My Life (live)/Now I'm Here (live)
EMI 2959. Released 29 June 1979. Reached No 63

Crazy Little Thing Called Love/We Will Rock You (live)
EMI 5001. Released 5 October 1979. Reached No 2

Save Me/Let Me Entertain You (live)
EMI 5022. Released 25 January 1980. Reached No 11

Play The Game/A Human Body
EMI 5076. Released 30 May 1980. Reached No 14

Another One Bites The Dust/Dragon Attack
EMI 5102. Released 22 August 1980. Reached No 7

Flash/Football Fight
EMI 5126. Released 24 November 1980. Reached No 10

Under Pressure/Soul Brother
EMI 5250. Released 26 October 1981. Reached No 1

Body Language/Life Is Real (Song For Lennon)
EMI 5293. Released 19 April 1982. Reached No 25

Las Palabras De Amor (The Words Of Love)/Cool Cat
EMI 5316. Released 1 June 1982. Reached No 17

Back Chat (remix)/Staying Power
EMI 5325. Released 9 August 1982. Reached No 40

Radio Ga Ga/I Go Crazy
EMI QUEEN 1. Released 23 January 1984. Reached No 2

I Want To Break Free/Machines (Or Back To Humans)
EMI QUEEN 2. Released 2 April 1984. Reached No 3

It's A Hard Life/Is This The World We Created?
EMI QUEEN 3. Released 16 July 1984. Reached No 6

Hammer To Fall (edit)/Tear It Up
EMI QUEEN 4. Released 10 September 1984. Reached No 13

Thank God It's Christmas/Man On The Prowl/Keep Passing The Open Windows
EMI QUEEN 5. Released 26 November 1984. Reached No 21

One Vision/Blurred Vision
EMI QUEEN 6. Released 4 November 1985. Reached No 7

A Kind Of Magic/A Dozen Red Roses For My Darling
EMI QUEEN 7. Released 17 March 1986. Reached No 3

Friends Will Be Friends/Seven Seas Of Rhye
EMI QUEEN 8. Released 9 June 1986. Reached No 14

Who Wants To Live Forever/Killer Queen
EMI QUEEN 9. Released 15 September 1986. Reached No 24

I Want It All/Hang On In There
Parlophone QUEEN 10. Released 2 May 1989. Reached No 3

Breakthru/Stealin'
Parlophone QUEEN 11. Released 19 June 1989. Reached No 7

The Invisible Man/Hijack My Heart
Parlophone QUEEN 12. Released 7 August 1989. Reached No 12

Scandal/My Life Has Been Saved
Parlophone QUEEN 14. Released 9 October 1989. Reached No 25

The Miracle/Stone Cold Crazy (live)
Parlophone QUEEN 15. Released 27 November 1989. Reached No 21

Innuendo/Bijou
Parlophone QUEEN 16. Released 14 January 1991. Reached No 1

I'm Going Slightly Mad/The Hitman
Parlophone QUEEN 17. Released 4 March 1991. Reached No 22

Headlong/All God's People
Parlophone QUEEN 18. Released 13 May 1991. Reached No 14

The Show Must Go On/Keep Yourself Alive
Parlophone QUEEN 19. Released 14 October 1991. Reached No 16

Bohemian Rhapsody/These Are The Days Of Our Lives (double A-side)
Parlophone QUEEN 20. Released 9 December 1991. Reached No 1